Iris Carlton-LaNey
N. Yolanda Burwell
Editors

African American Community Practice Models: Historical and Contemporary Responses

Pre-publication REVIEWS, COMMENTARIES, EVALUATIONS . . .

This book is significant for the social work profession since it acknowledges the long neglected contributions of African Americans to the development of social welfare in the U.S. generally, and their contributions to community practice in particular.

The revitalization of community practice in the social work profession is much overdue. Its resurgence is critical for responding to community problems as we approach the millennium. This book, no doubt, will help us face the challenge in an inclusive and empowering fashion. Students, teachers, practitioners, policymakers, and others interested in social welfare, especially communities, are urged to read it.

Bogart R. Leashore, PhD
Dean and Professor, Hunter College School of Social Work

T his small and packed volume provides powerful lessons from the past and guides to the future. The two historical entries provide important and little known facts about social work's roots in the African-American community. More importantly, within this context of history, there resides an important critique of social work's professional claims to social justice. Too often there is a blanket assumption and/or uncritical view that social work has always "done the right thing." The two entries by Burwell and Carlton-Laney remind us that our profession is not immune to the social forces that often serve to promote injustice rather than social justice and in these records is revealed an inspiring account of individuals who as social workers without a professional support context managed to persevere and provide significant contributions to their communities and therefore the entire nation. Finally, these entries remind us that it is often from long term, undramatic efforts that significant and lasting progress is established. The further power of these entries lies in the fact that they are good history first and through this lens the authors challenge us to evaluate our present as well.

T he entries focusing on current community practice efforts are timely both in that they address challenging problems and they also serve as models to guide others. Meeting the challenge of HIV/AIDS is daunting to us all, but each community, ethnic or otherwise, must struggle with many nuances that further complicate matters. The continuing struggle for communities to provide constructive outlets for youth is fraught with major challenges given the increase in the level of violence among adolescents and young adults. In both cases, whether HIV/AIDS or the new challenges of youth violence, the examples of community practice provided here offer a renewed perspective on this important area of social work.

Gary R. Lowe, PhD
Dean, School of Social Work
East Carolina University

This volume is an important contribution to the ongoing effort to expand the official account of social work past and present. The authors have done an outstanding job of documenting the presence and work of African Americans in social work during the Progressive Era and currently. Forerunners of social work, Lawrence Oxley, Ida B. Wells-Barnett and Lugenia Burns Hope are highlighted. Their work established state run programming, contributed to community social work practice theory and set the direction for early social work education. Professionally trained social workers, George and Birdye Haynes, executed programs which laid the foundation for the modern day examples included in this book. A major point made in this book and woven into each chapter is that the role of community practitioners in African American communities must be decidedly different. The social work reformist thrust of applying public solutions to community problems must be replaced by a commitment to building institutions.

Tawana Ford Sabbath, MSS, PhD
Adjunct Faculty, Covenant International Institute

For a number of years, social workers and historians have been exploring the development of self-help and advocacy programs among African Americans, topics which have been neglected by social workers and historians alike. The editors have selected essays which examine these topics and apply them to present-day concerns in community practice.

I would recommend this book as a supplemental text in courses on community organization/macro social work practice. The essays will relate the content of these courses to working in African American communities. In addition, because of its good coverage of the Progressive era and the 1920s, this book would be an excellent supplemental text for courses on the history of social work. The book might also be useful as a text for a course on minority issues in social work.

I am happy to have had the opportunity to review this book. It is a valuable contribution to the literature of social work history as well as the literature of community organization practice.

Paul H. Stuart, PhD
Professor, School of Social Work, The University of Alabama

This collection of well-documented articles, informed both by solid historiography and a deeply humane perspective, accomplishes a number of important purposes and does so very well. It helps to remedy a regrettable neglect of the history of social welfare programs, many of them staffed by skilled professionals, in the African-American community. It helps to balance the scales of memory while emphasizing strengths exhibited in the past and, in the case of the article by Farrell and his colleagues, the present.

If you're a social worker who cares about today's and tomorrow's African-American communities, read this book. If you're a teacher of social work–or of twentieth-century American social history–teach from this book. If you're a student, you can learn a great deal both about Community Practice and about the value of historical research from it. It is likely to become a classic in its own right.

Paul H. Ephross, PhD
Professor, School of Social Work,
University of Maryland at Baltimore

At a time when social work must reassess both strategy and tactics to accomplish its mission, this book emphasizes the importance of community-based approaches in working with African Americans. Utilizing historical studies and analyses of contemporary programs, the book expands on an old social work maxim and argues that the most effective practice begins "where the consumers of service are."

This book represents cutting-edge scholarship which reemphasizes the importance of community practice in working for the betterment of populations who are often seen as having intractable social problems because of high rates of individual pathology. It is a welcome antidote to the naysayers who suggest that the African American community is shattered and that community approaches to problem resolution are difficult if not impossible.

John M. Herrick, PhD
Professor and Associate Director,
School of Social Work, Michigan
State University

African American Community Practice Models: Historical and Contemporary Responses

African American Community Practice Models: Historical and Contemporary Responses

Iris Carlton-LaNey, PhD
N. Yolanda Burwell, PhD
Editors

Routledge
Taylor & Francis Group

LONDON AND NEW YORK

African American Community Practice Models: Historical and Contemporary Responses has also been published as *Journal of Community Practice*, Volume 2, Number 4 1995.

First published 1996 by The Haworth Press, Inc.

2 Park Square, Milton Park, Abingdon, Oxon OX14 4RN
711 Third Avenue, New York, NY 10017, USA

Routledge is an imprint of the Taylor & Francis Group, an informa business

First issued in paperback 2016

Library of Congress Cataloging-in-Publication Data

African American community practice models : historical and contemporary responses / Iris Carlton-LaNey, N. Yolanda Burwell, editors.
     p. cm.
     " 'African American community practice models : historical and contemporary responses' has
also been published as 'Journal of Community Practice', Volume 2, Number 4 1995".
     Includes bibliographical references (p.) and index.
     1. Afro-Americans–Social conditions. 2. Community organization–United States. I. Carlton-
LaNey, Iris. II. Burwell, N. Yolanda. III. Journal of community practice.
E185.86.A3315 1996
305.896'073–dc20   96-12676
                                                                  CIP

ISBN 13: 978-1-56024-791-3 (hbk)
ISBN 13: 978-1-138-96625-3 (pbk)

INDEXING & ABSTRACTING

Contributions to this publication are selectively indexed or abstracted in print, electronic, online, or CD-ROM version(s) of the reference tools and information services listed below. This list is current as of the copyright date of this publication. See the end of this section for additional notes.

- *Alternative Press Index,* Alternative Press Center, Inc., P.O. Box 33109, Baltimore, MD 21218-0401

- *Applied Social Sciences Index & Abstracts (ASSIA) (Online: ASSI via Data-Star) (CDRom: ASSIA Plus),* Bowker-Saur Limited, Maypole House, Maypole Road, East Grinstead, West Sussex RH19 1HH, England

- *caredata CD: the social and community care database,* National Institute for Social Work, 5 Tavistock Place, London WC1H 9SS, England

- *CNPIEC Reference Guide: Chinese National Directory of Foreign Periodicals,* P.O. Box 88, Beijing, People's Republic of China

- *CPcurrents,* ITServices, 3301 Alta Arden #3, Sacramento, CA 95825

- *Economic Literature Index (Journal of Economic Literature) print version plus OnLine Abstracts (on Dialog) plus EconLit on CD-ROM (American Economic Association),* American Economic Association Publication, 4615 Fifth Avenue, Pittsburgh, PA 15213-3661

- *Family Studies Database (online and CD/ROM),* Peters Technology Transfer, 306 East Baltimore Pike, 2nd Floor, Media, PA 19063

- *Family Violence & Sexual Assault Bulletin,* Family Violence & Sexual Assault Institute, 1310 Clinic Drive, Tyler, TX 75701

- *Guide to Social Science & Religion in Periodical Literature,* National Periodical Library, P.O. Box 3278, Clearwater, FL 34630

(continued)

- *Human Resources Abstracts (HRA),* Sage Publications, Inc., 2455 Teller Road, Newbury Park, CA 91320

- *IBZ International Bibliography of Periodical Literature,* Zeller Verlag GmbH & Co., P.O.B. 1949, d-49009 Osnabruck, Germany

- *Index to Periodical Articles Related to Law,* University of Texas, 727 East 26th Street, Austin, TX 78705

- *International Political Science Abstracts,* 27 Rue Saint-Guillaume, F-75337 Paris, Cedex 07, France

- *INTERNET ACCESS (& additional networks) Bulletin Board for Libraries ("BUBL"), coverage of information resources on INTERNET, JANET, and other networks.*
  - JANET X. 29: UK.AC.BATH.BUBL or 00006012101300
  - TELNET: BUBL.BATH.AC.UK or 138.38.32.45 login 'bubl'
  - Gopher: BUBL.BATH.AC.UK (138.32.32.45). Port 7070
  - World Wide Web: http://www.bubl.bath.ac.uk./BUBL/home.html
  - NISSWAIS: telnetniss.ac.uk (for the NISS gateway)
  The Andersonian Library, Curran Building, 101 St. James Road, Glasgow G4 ONS, Scotland

- *National Library Database on Homelessness,* National Coalition for the Homeless, 1612 K Street, NW, #1004, Homelessness Information Exchange, Washington, DC 20006

- *Operations Research/Management Science,* Executive Sciences Institute, 1005 Mississippi Avenue, Davenport, IA 52803

- *Public Affairs Information Bulletin (PAIS),* Public Affairs Information Service, Inc., 521 West 43rd Street, New York, NY 10036-4396

- *Rural Development Abstracts (CAB Abstracts), c/o CAB International/CAB ACCESS . . . available in print, diskettes updated weekly, and on INTERNET. Providing full bibliographic listings, author affiliation, augmented keyword searching.* CAB International, Wallingford Oxon OX10 8DE, United Kingdom

- *Sage Family Studies Abstracts (SFSA),* Sage Publications, Inc., 2455 Teller Road, Newbury Park, CA 91320

(continued)

- *Social Work Abstracts,* National Association of Social Workers, 750 First Street NW, 8th Floor, Washington, DC 20002

- *Sociological Abstracts (SA),* Sociological Abstracts, Inc., P.O. Box 22206, San Diego, CA 92192-0206

- *Transportation Research Abstracts,* National Research Council, 2101 Constitution Avenue NW, GR314, Washington, DC 20418

- *Urban Affairs Abstracts,* National League of Cities, 1301 Pennsylvania Avenue NW, Washington, DC 20004

SPECIAL BIBLIOGRAPHIC NOTES

related to special journal issues (separates)
and indexing/abstracting

❑ indexing/abstracting services in this list will also cover material in any "separate" that is co-published simultaneously with Haworth's special thematic journal issue or DocuSerial. Indexing/abstracting usually covers material at the article/chapter level.

❑ monographic co-editions are intended for either non-subscribers or libraries which intend to purchase a second copy for their circulating collections.

❑ monographic co-editions are reported to all jobbers/wholesalers/approval plans. The source journal is listed as the "series" to assist the prevention of duplicate purchasing in the same manner utilized for books-in-series.

❑ to facilitate user/access services all indexing/abstracting services are encouraged to utilize the co-indexing entry note indicated at the bottom of the first page of each article/chapter/contribution.

❑ this is intended to assist a library user of any reference tool (whether print, electronic, online, or CD-ROM) to locate the monographic version if the library has purchased this version but not a subscription to the source journal.

❑ individual articles/chapters in any Haworth publication are also available through the Haworth Document Delivery Services (HDDS).

ABOUT THE EDITORS

Iris B. Carlton-LaNey, PhD, is Associate Professor in the School of Social Work at the University of North Carolina at Chapel Hill. She has been teaching courses in several areas of social work for 20 years. The author of *Elderly Black Farm Women as Keepers of the Community and the Culture,* Dr. Carlton-LaNey has written numerous book chapters and articles on topics including aging African American women in the South, the education of homeless children, and African Americans working in social work.

N. Yolanda Burwell, PhD, is Assistant Professor in the School of Social Work at East Carolina University in Greenville, North Carolina. She is the founder of Salt of the Earth, a small historical research firm which conducted a historical study of the first three African American women attorneys in North Carolina and also retails and brokers African American cultural products. Dr. Burwell's research interests include social welfare history in African American communities, early Black female leaders and organizations, and the ways and means by which African Americans have engaged in self-help and empowerment activities. She is a reputable consultant/trainer for human services agencies in North Carolina, conducting workshops on teamwork, communication, problem-solving, and empowerment.

African American
Community Practice Models:
Historical and Contemporary
Responses

CONTENTS

Introduction:
African American
Community Practice Models:
Historical and Contemporary Responses

Iris Carlton-LaNey, PhD
N. Yolanda Burwell, PhD

This volume focuses on community practice among African Americans in both an historical and present day context. Several recurring themes emerge in this collection. First, the primacy of respecting the African American culture resonates throughout each author's discussion. The importance of this aspect of African Ameri-́can community practice cannot be underestimated. Second, the articles included in this book focus on the need "to begin where the community is" and to understand the community in order to develop appropriate services and programs, to advocate successfully, and to build social and political power. Finally, these authors suggest that it is important to focus on the "collectivity," or the interdependence and group identity that flow from the African tradition and are an integral part of the African American community.

The historical articles in this volume provide excellent content on pioneer community practice encompassing elements of advocacy, human social and economic development, social justice, and political and social action. New historical content is introduced, present- ing social work leaders and personalities who must be brought back

[Haworth co-indexing entry note]: "Introduction: African American Community Practice Models: Historical and Contemporary Responses." Carlton-LaNey, Iris, and N. Yolanda Burwell. Co-published simultaneously in *Journal of Community Practice* (The Haworth Press, Inc.) Vol. 2, No. 4, 1995, pp. 1-6; and: *African American Community Practice Models: Historical and Contemporary Responses* (ed: Iris Carlton-LaNey, and N. Yolanda Burwell) The Haworth Press, Inc., 1996, pp. 1-6. Single or multiple copies of this article are available from The Haworth Document Delivery Service [1-800-342-9678, 9:00 a.m. - 5:00 p.m. (EST)].

from obscurity. Their contributions to community practice, planning, and policy development at the local, state, and national levels during times of strict segregation and desegregation are fascinating lessons in resourcefulness and tenacity among pioneer social workers. Essentially, these articles help to correct the historical record with regard to African American social work/welfare as well as to give models of community practice which are relevant today. Thematically and historically "race work" or work for the sociopolitical inclusion of African Americans is at the foundation of community practice among this population. Many of the same social problems of racism, segregation in housing, insufficient services, and inadequate open and honest communication continue today as in the past. The authors echo one another in their focus on this historical and contemporary phenomena.

The approaches that our pioneer social workers and social welfare leaders used continue to be relevant to the struggles for social justice, equity, and effective community practice today. The historical articles in this collection provide a framework for practice that the authors focusing on contemporary issues utilize as they discuss practice strategies such as midnight basketball and services to stop the spread of AIDS. The authors examine, describe and introduce proactive and innovative community initiatives/strategies which respond directly to the culture and lifestyles of African Americans. The continuity of this dimension over time and circumstance begins to really speak to an internal, yet often unspoken, legacy among African American social workers to practice social work in a different and more affirming way when clients are African Americans. Practice from a strengths perspective overrides the notion of pathology and deficit which permeates social work literature where African Americans are concerned. These writers' works recognize the humaneness as well as the distinctiveness of culture. Whether working in early social settlement houses, organizing to hire African American social workers, or developing a midnight basketball league, community work is tailored to African American lifestyles, needs, and capabilities. Rather than blaming the victims of historical or modern oppression, these authors remind us of the internal capabilities which emerge or can develop when working at the community level. The profession's preoccupation with individual irresponsibilities and maladjustments ignores the "potentials" for positive and planned change at the community level. It is clear from the content in this volume that a return to community intervention is both imperative and timely.

Sandra O'Donnell's article, "Urban African American Community Development in the Progressive Era," presents a broad overview of organized social activism on the part of two Progressive Era reformers, Lugenia Burns Hope and Ida B. Wells-Barnett. Two major community development strategies, social betterment and social protest, provide the framework for her discussion. While neither Wells-Barnett nor Hope were professionally trained social workers, their work reflected the social welfare and community practice work typical among African Americans during the early part of this century. In identifying broad community development matters and social problems, the author indicates specific strategies that Wells-Barnett and Hope (as well as others) used to tackle the problems that plagued African American communities in urban areas. O'Donnell also alerts us to the use of social research to guide community practice interventions and concludes by urging us to engage in further research to identify the pioneers and their methods of practice in a hostile society which continues to deny them their place in social work's history.

"George and Birdye Haynes' Legacy to Community Practice," by Iris Carlton-LaNey, presents the community practice work of a brother-sister team of professionally trained social work reformers. As graduates from the New York School of Philanthropy and the Chicago School of Civics and Philanthropy, respectively, George and Birdye Haynes engaged in social work which focused on the community as they saw it. The rules of both physical and social segregation that placed the Hayneses within the same physical space as those whom they served helped to ensure that their work was both sensitive and appropriately targeted. Through descriptions of the Haynes' efforts in the National Urban League, the Fisk University Department of Social Sciences, the Wendell Phillips Settlement in Chicago, and Lincoln House Settlement in New York, Carlton-LaNey presents a picture of local, regional, and national community practice which focused on a range of activities and programs. The need to see the African American community thrive, to enhance the quality of life of residents moving into cities in the north and south, and to train African American professional social workers for practice among their people, provided much of the impetus for the Haynes' work. Both George and Birdye Haynes engaged in myriad projects that acknowledged the community's weaknesses but focused on its strengths. Their legacy to the social work profession and community practice can provide useful information for educators and practitioners alike as they search for ways and means to meet the needs of communities today.

N. Yolanda Burwell's article, "Lawrence Oxley and Locality Development: Black Self-Help in North Carolina 1925-1928," presents the intense social work and institution building of one pioneer social welfare leader on a state level. Burwell describes Oxley's community organizing approach and his work in three of North Carolina's larger counties. Oxley contributed to the development of professional social work practice by establishing a state social welfare agency concerned with the needs of African Americans, by promoting social work education and training for African Americans through public welfare institutes, and by organizing African American citizens to remedy pressing social welfare needs at the local level. Burwell gives specific historical information, using primary data, to illustrate African American social welfare and self-help in North Carolina. Oxley's exacting techniques for organizing and locality development are discussed along with his service integration efforts which identified and helped with the development and maintenance of numerous other social welfare organizations. Burwell concludes that Oxley advanced community organizing as a viable social work methodology when it was just emerging as a distinct social work intervention.

In advocating for risk reduction behavior changes, Irene Luckey's article, "HIV/AIDS Prevention in the African American Community: An Integrated Community-Based Practice Approach," offers a new and timely look at strategies to eliminate the transmittal of this deadly disease. Luckey takes the position that the situational and environmental context of African Americans' lives, and their responses to HIV/AIDS, should be incorporated into HIV prevention/education programs. The author offers a multi-level system intervention approach grounded in an ecosystem perspective that focuses on the community as the target of intervention in work with African Americans. Luckey further discusses factors that affect African Americans' response to HIV/AIDS and uses that as a springboard for developing a more responsive approach to HIV prevention in the African American community. She discusses the types of barriers that social workers must overcome in their work within the community, the need for community awareness that is culture-specific, and the informal mechanisms for gaining community support and access to community leadership. The author cites the community forum as one mechanism for open and frank discussions in a safe environment. Furthermore, according to Luckey, the integrated practice approach provides an opportunity for the church and other community groups to become involved in problem-solving around difficult and emotionally charged topics, such as AIDS, without becoming initiators. Luckey concludes that this type of community effort can lead to linkages or coalitions which may help the community to address other problems.

The article written by Walter C. Farrell, James H. Johnson, Marty Sapp, Roger M. Pumphrey, and Shirley Freeman entitled "Redirecting the Lives of Urban Black Males: An Assessment of Milwaukee's Midnight Basketball League" provides a comprehensive evaluation of the effectiveness of Milwaukee's midnight basketball program. The authors describe the program as part of a new generation of social resources for inner city communities. Funded entirely by the private sector, the league, like other midnight basketball leagues in the country, was designed to serve as an alternative to drugs, gangs, and violence for young adult males in Milwaukee. An evaluation survey was developed and administered to a 60% sample of league participants during the last three days of the 1992-93 season. The results of the survey indicated that the program created a safe haven for participants to engage in social activities, positively channeled the gang members' energy, and significantly improved the educational and career aspirations of program participants. This article reminds us of the important role that organized recreation has historically served for urban dwellers. One of the most salient points of the article is that it describes a service which corresponds to the lifestyles of young adults in center cities. Rather than making these young men adapt to an existing service system, the system changed to attend to the particular needs of this unique population. The authors' conclusion suggests that a community based program developed from a strengths perspective and tailored to meet the needs of a specific population, was a worthwhile investment in human capital which far exceeded the initial cash outlay.

Finally, if social work professes to embrace diversity and an understanding of difference, it must strengthen and expand its knowledge of African American social welfare history. Lacking this knowledge makes it very difficult, if not impossible, for us to develop services and programs that are culturally sensitive and community responsive. Collectively and individually, these authors have helped us to fulfill our professional obligation "to know." Hopefully, publications such as this signal the continued investment and commitment to reexamine social welfare history, making it more inclusive as we meet future challenges of social reform.

Urban African American Community Development in the Progressive Era

Sandra M. O'Donnell, PhD

SUMMARY. This article describes community development efforts in urban African American communities in the Progressive era. It features the work of Ida B. Wells-Barnett, who mobilized people to protest for equal rights and justice, and Lugenia Burns Hope, whose Neighborhood Union was a model of organization for social support and policy change. Other efforts for "social betterment" and "social protest" are described. African American community activism was distinguished by its emphases on community building—encompassing physical, human, and social capital—and on securing justice for black citizens. The article concludes with implications for modern day community organization/development theory and practice. *[Article copies available from The Haworth Document Delivery Service: 1-800-342-9678.]*

KEYWORDS. African American, community building, progressive era, community development, community organizing

The community organization and development literature is largely ahistorical. The few histories that do exist are truncated, tracing the "roots" of community organization to the originating

---

Sandra M. O'Donnell is Associate Professor in Public Administration at Roosevelt University in Chicago, IL.

Address correspondence to: Sandra O'Donnell, Associate Professor, Public Administration, Roosevelt University, 430 S. Michigan, #760, Chicago, IL 60605.

[Haworth co-indexing entry note]: "Urban African American Community Development in the Progressive Era." O'Donnell, Sandra M. Co-published simultaneously in *Journal of Community Practice* (The Haworth Press, Inc.) Vol. 2, No. 4, 1995, pp. 7-26; and: *African American Community Practice Models: Historical and Contemporary Responses* (ed: Iris Carlton-LaNey, and N. Yolanda Burwell) The Haworth Press, Inc., 1996, pp. 7-26. Single or multiple copies of this article are available from The Haworth Document Delivery Service [1-800-342-9678, 9:00 a.m. - 5:00 p.m. (EST)].

institutions of professional social work, the charity organization societies, and the settlements (Betten & Austin, 1990; Burghardt,1987; Fisher & Romanofsky, 1981; Kramer & Specht, 1975). This approach may be valid in tracing the development of community organization and community development as fields of social work practice, but it excludes thought and experience outside the professional social work tradition that might inform theory and practice. This article is one beginning effort to expand our knowledge of the history of community practice by focusing on urban African American organizers in the Progressive era. The work of two women, Ida B. Wells-Barnett and Lugenia Burns Hope, is examined, and the use of two major community building strategies—social betterment and social protest—by African American organizers is described.

The focus on the Progressive Era (roughly, 1900-1917) is *not* an attempt to locate the origins of African American community building. Blacks had been involved in organizing community self-help institutions, as well as passive and active resistance to slavery and other forms of racial injustice, long before then (see Bibliographic Note). Rather, this article focuses on the Progressive Era because a variety of conditions and events converged then to create a climate for a period of intense community building activities (see Bibliographic Note). Salient conditions included: the rapid urbanization of Black America, increased social stratification within the African American community, increased segregation accompanied by declining living conditions for African Americans, the rise of dense ghettos in urban areas, and a rich ideological debate between accomodationists like Booker T. Washington and integrationists like W.E.B. DuBois (as well as nationalists like Marcus Garvey) that fueled local reform efforts.

A note on definitions. This article uses the term "community building" to describe a variety of community practice methods our African American forebears employed to improve the quality of life in their communities, including neighborhood and community organizing, functional community organizing, community social and economic development, program development and community liaison, political and social action, and social movements (Weil & Gamble, 1995).

Finally, a note on limitations. This paper is a review of secondary source information only. It represents a *beginning* step to incorporate African American history into the knowledge base of community practice. It is offered to (1) make the historical literature accessible to community practitioners and students, and (2) spur scholars to pursue additional knowledge and theory building using primary sources.

TWO PROGRESSIVE ERA AFRICAN AMERICAN COMMUNITY ORGANIZERS

Two women–Ida B. Wells-Barnett and Lugenia Burns Hope–illustrate the creativity, richness, and diversity of African American community building efforts in the Progressive Era. These women are perhaps atypical from other Black organizers in the magnitude of their impact, but they are also in many ways representative of the cadre of Black community activists of their era. Both were married to prominent men; both also had children. Like most other African American activists, both had higher educations, at a time when fewer than 1% of Blacks did. And, in contrast to most White activists, both emphasized self-help rather than increased public responsibility.

Ida B. Wells-Barnett's Community Work

Ida B. Wells-Barnett was a journalist who became an internationally recognized activist for anti-lynching legislation and for equal rights and justice more generally (Duster, 1970; Lerner, 1974; Peebles-Wilkins & Francis, 1990; Spear, 1967). She was also a community organizer *par excellence.* While a publisher of Memphis' Black weekly, *Free Speech,* she singlehandedly initiated a Black boycott of White businesses, as well as a Black exodus from Memphis, in response to the city's indifference to the lynching of three of her friends. So successful was her campaign that "leading citizens" of Memphis destroyed her office and left a death threat. As a result of a fundraiser held by New York women activists to aid Wells, clubs were soon organized in New York (DuBois, 1909; Duster, 1970; Lerner, 1974) and Boston (Duster, 1970; Giddings, 1984) to further the anti-lynching cause as well as other civil rights issues. These efforts proved to be the beginning of the burgeoning African American women's club movement, which became the National Association of Colored Women's Clubs in 1896 and soon claimed 50,000 members in over 1,000 clubs nationwide (Duster, 1970; Giddings, 1984; Lerner, 1974). As Paula Giddings (1974, p. 94) notes, Wells' anti-lynching campaign "brought Black women into the forefront of the struggle for Black and women's rights."

After touring England to muster up support for her anti-lynching crusade, Ida B. Wells went to Chicago, initially to raise money for a pamphlet she was to publish protesting the lack of attention to Blacks at the 1893 World's Fair. She decided to stay there, "to make Chicago my home and develop the newly established women's clubs" (Duster, 1970, p. 122) and got a job at the city's leading African American newspaper, *The Conservator.* She founded the first Black women's club in the city, which soon boasted 300 members, sponsored speakers on issues of concern to Blacks, raised money to aid in the prosecution of a policeman who had killed an African American, organized a local anti-lynching campaign, and sponsored a kindergarten.

The next years of Ida B. Wells' life were largely focused on marriage (to Ferdinand Barnett, publisher of *The Conservator*), motherhood, and national level work in the anti-lynching crusade and the formation of the Afro-American Council. Through the Council, she became a nationally recognized, outspoken opponent of Booker T. Washington's accomodationism (Peebles-Wilkins & Francis, 1990; Spear, 1967). She remained involved at the local level in the organization of an interracial countywide federation of women's clubs, in organizing a committee (chaired by Jane Addams) to force *The Tribune* to abandon its campaign to segregate the public schools, and, for a time, in helping organize the Frederick Douglass Settlement House, which was founded and run by White people to promote interracial understanding (Duster, 1970 and Spear, 1967). Wells-Barnett broke with the group when its leadership publicly suggested that Black criminality (rather than White racism) fueled lynchings.

She returned to grassroots community work through her church in 1908. When women's and other civic clubs failed to act in response to the Springfield, Illinois race riot, she vented her frustration to her Sunday men's Bible class. Immediately she organized them into a Sunday afternoon club where they "discussed matters affecting race," proceeded to take them to Joliet prison to "begin some practical studies," and subsequently mobilized them to open a storefront on State Street (the vice district) to provide "uplift" to deter Black men from criminal activity (Duster, 1970, p. 300). This group, named the Negro Fellowship League, became a social service and employment center that served as a prototype for the Chicago Urban League (Duster, 1970; Spear, 1967). The group also became the organizing base for Wells-Barnett's continuing protests–against unfair treatment of Blacks in World War I and in response to the East St. Louis race riot of 1918 (Duster, 1970; Tuttle, 1977)–as well as a Sunday afternoon religious-based discussion club. Unlike most other Black civic groups, the League was not controlled by "leading citizens;" its officers included men employed as an elevator operator, a redcap, and a rag picker.

In later years, Wells-Barnett organized two additional local organizations (Giddings, 1984)–a women's suffrage organization and a protective association for Blacks. Ida B. Wells-Barnett organized for nearly 40 years. She fought racial injustice at both the local and national levels, and played a critical role in the emergence of the Black women's club movement. Her most ardently fought battle, the anti-lynching cause, failed to secure national legislation, but Wells-Barnett *did* halt the practice in Illinois, and her work laid the ground for subsequent NAACP attempts to pass federal anti-lynching legislation (Duster, 1970; Franklin, 1980). Wells-Barnett's organizing style combined meticulous research (a Progressive Era hallmark) with dogged determination, public speaking talent, and an apparent fearlessness in taking radical positions on issues affecting African Americans (Giddings, 1984; Peebles-Wilkins & Francis, 1990).

LUGENIA BURNS HOPE'S NEIGHBORHOOD UNION

Lugenia Burns Hope became familiar with neighborhood activism as an adolescent in Chicago, when she worked at Hull House. When she moved to Atlanta in 1898 with her husband, John Hope, who was to take an academic position at Atlanta Baptist (Morehouse) College, she immediately got involved in organizing a conference on child welfare, in establishing a day nursery association, and in establishing the first playground for Black children in the city. In response to the death of a young woman in the neighborhood in 1908, Mrs. Hope organized a survey of service needs, and, subsequently, created the Neighborhood Union to meet those needs. The Union had broad aims—to provide playgrounds and service centers, to promote neighborliness, to increase cleanliness, to promote child welfare, to suppress vice and crime, and to impart the cultural heritage of the African American community to its members (Lerner, 1974; Pollard, 1978; Rouse, 1984; Rouse, 1989; Shivery, 1936; Scott, 1990).

The Neighborhood Union's tightly planned neighborhood organizing structure (Rouse,1984; Shivery, 1936) pre-dated the better known Cincinnati Social Unit experiment (Betten & Austin, 1990) by nearly ten years. ". . . [R]ecognizing that all reform works better when the people involved are an integral part of the planning" (Scott, 1990, p.14), the Neighborhood Union organized its work in neighborhood and sub-neighborhood (district) units. Each district was supervised by a team of a neighborhood president and a neighborhood director. The neighborhood president was a resident who organized her district, leading home improvement, street clean-up, and anti-tuberculosis campaigns. The neighborhood director was a Neighborhood Union co-founder, often a Morehouse faculty wife, who was responsible for periodic door-to-door surveys and for acquainting residents with plans for neighborhood improvement.

The district directors comprised the Board of Directors of the Neighborhood Union. A Board of Managers, comprised of the district presidents, zone directors (multiple districts), and department heads (arts, health, education, and the like) set program and policy directions for the Union (Rouse, 1984). Classes, clubs, and events were held in facilities throughout the districts until the Neighborhood Union bought a building in 1922 "which became the center for its varied activities" (Lerner, 1974, p. 105).

The Neighborhood Union tackled social problems in the Black community through a combination of research, outreach, education, direct service provision, and activism. An example of this approach was the Union's early efforts to improve the health of Black Atlantans. A door-to-door survey in 1908 uncovered serious health problems. With these findings, the Union "petitioned the mayor, the city council, and the sanitation and health departments to improve present facilities" (Rouse, 1984, p. 121). Instead, responsibility for public health services in the Black community was turned over to the Union, which set up a clinic and public education programs. Available evidence suggests small sums of public and philanthropic dollars accompanied this policy shift, but in amounts wholly insufficient to meet the community's needs, for the Union energetically raised funds within the African American community for its public health programs.

A similar strategy was used to confront the tuberculosis problem in 1914. Using the Union's district structure, a committee was appointed to survey sanitary conditions in homes and the schools. As a result, a black branch of the Anti-Tuberculosis Association was created in 1915, to provide a visiting nurse service and public education programs (Pollard, 1978; Rouse, 1984).

Another Union concern was the city's Black schools. A survey of them in 1913 revealed tremendous overcrowding, dilapidated facilities, poorly paid teachers, and double sessions. Neighborhood Union agitation resulted in the building of a new school, increasing teachers' salaries, and getting the school Board to permit the use of schools as neighborhood centers; conditions, however, still remained severely substandard (Pollard, 1978; Rouse, 1984; Shivery, 1936).

Lugenia Burns Hope led the Union's efforts to get African Americans hired as policemen (the campaign failed), to educate the community to participate in the Census, to petition the city for better parks and police protection, to eliminate double shifts in Black schools, to petition the schools for free kindergartens and for truant officers, to campaign for better public transportation and social services in the African American community, and to improve the infrastructure of Black neighborhoods. Mrs. Hope also spearheaded the establishment of what would become the Atlanta School of Social Work, chaired the National Association of Colored Women's Clubs committees on neighborhoods and citizenship, and campaigned for women's suffrage (Lerner, 1974; Giddings, 1984; Pollard, 1978; Rouse, 1984; Rouse, 1989).

Lugenia Burns Hope fought for racial justice at the regional and national levels. She helped organize White and Black women's clubs in the South to work together on the anti-lynching issue. And she spearheaded a successful nationwide campaign to secure the right of African American women to select YWCA staff in their communities. Gerda Lerner (1974, p. 166) wrote of Burns Hope: "This dynamic leader, characteristic of her generation, worked in a quiet, behind-the-scenes way. Yet her leadership spirit generated not only a remarkable local reform drive, but moved on to the national scene." Mrs. Hope led the Neighborhood Union for 30 years, before widowhood, declining health, and a conflict with Morehouse College precipitated a move North (Rouse, 1989).

TWO MAJOR COMMUNITY DEVELOPMENT STRATEGIES– SOCIAL BETTERMENT AND SOCIAL PROTEST

The work of Ida B. Wells-Barnett and Lugenia Burns Hope illustrates the variety of community practice methods undertaken in the Progressive Era to build the African American community. These combined methods had a dual focus–building or strengthening institutions and "social bonds" (Williams, 1905) within the African American community, and eliminating injustices in the wider society that affected the vitality of African American communities. The term used at the time for the former set of activities was "social betterment;" for the latter set, "social protest." In modern community practice terminology (Weil & Gamble, 1995), "social betterment" activities would largely embrace both the community social and economic development model (developing local leadership and mutual support, building local institutions with or without external finance), and the program development and community liaison model (expanding and improving community programs). "Social protest" activities would embrace the neighborhood and community organizing model (developing local capacity to change external institutions), organizing functional communities (in national level campaigns, African Americans were the defined "community"), political and social action (building political power to change public policy), and social movements (creating new visions for social justice in behalf of a particular group).

Social Betterment

With burgeoning populations and declining access to White social institutions, the Progressive Era witnessed a proliferation of Black self-help and mutual aid activities (see Bibliographic Note). Like ethnic White community groups, Black community practice focused on institution building. This focus was in contrast to that of many White Progressive reform leaders, whose attention had turned to the development of public sector solutions to community problems (Gordon, 1991).

In cities throughout the North and South, African Americans established hospitals, clinics, schools, kindergartens, Y's, homes for single working women, day nurseries, orphanages, mutual benefit societies (later, insurance agencies) and old folks' homes. In some cases, these institutions were supported and controlled primarily by the African American community. These Black-controlled institutions were typically founded by women's clubs or by coalitions of women's clubs and businessmen. Fundraising for institutions in the Black community through benefits and individual donations was notoriously difficult and time-consuming. Some institutions turned to White philanthropists to survive, and lost Black control as a result. For example, Jane Hunter had difficulty sustaining the Phyllis Wheatley Home for working girls in Cleveland until a White philanthropist agreed to support it, but under the condition that White women be placed on the Board. In such cases, White interest in Black self-help served to reinforce Jim Crow segregation laws and discriminating customs (Kusmer, 1978).

African Americans adapted the social settlement movement to Black self-help, creating a rich variety of forms of settlements, some sponsored by churches, others organized by committed individuals, and others, by women's clubs. Many Black settlements emerged from the nineteenth century mission, which integrated church worship, schooling, social service, and social support (Lukar, 1984). Victoria Earle Mathews founded the White Rose Mission in 1897 or 1898 to provide shelter and "rescue" work for young Black girls who migrated to New York seeking employment;

the Mission later became a full-scale settlement, providing cultural, recreation, and educational programs as well as a kindergarten and mother's clubs (Lerner, 1974; Lukar, 1984).

Settlement-like programs were also sponsored by another descendant of the mission, the "institutional church" (Lukar, 1984). By 1910, Matthew Anderson's Berean Church in Philadephia had a medical dispensary, summer camp, two literary clubs, a WCTU chapter, an employment bureau, a kindergarten, youth programs, a building and loan association that had extended mortgages to 150 families, and a vocational school that served 1000 students. Hugh Proctor's First Congregational Church in Atlanta had women's and men's groups, a temperance program, and outreach missions in back alleys. Reverend Reverdy Ransom's Institutional Church and Social Settlement in Chicago had an employment bureau, a day nursery, a kindergarten, men's and women's clubs, programs for children, and an educational program.

African American community services were especially concerned with health, education, and employment (Gordon, 1991). Health conditions in Black communities were often so poor that an 1899 Atlanta University conference concluded, the "race could actually be destroyed" (Giddings, 1984). Efforts to improve sanitation in the home and in the community, to build healthcare institutions, and to develop health outreach programs thus had special import. In order to improve the local economy, campaigns were launched to encourage African American communities to patronize Black businesses. Jobs and the support of working people were seen as a critical community building tactic. Day nurseries (day care programs) and homes for working girls were more prominent in Black communities than in white ones. Job preparation and placement were the foci of the Negro Fellowship League and the national and local Urban Leagues. "Industrial and manual" schools to train young people in vocational occupations open to Blacks were a prominent program in many communities.

Like White social welfare institutions and settlements, most Black organizations were established by the middle class to serve the lower class (Giddings, 1985; Gordon, 1990; Scott, 1990). Why, then, the term "self-help"? The answer lies largely in a difference between the two races in impulse and in focus. With significant exceptions [for example, Jane Addams (1961) observed that settlement work gave one a sense of purpose], White volunteers and professionals largely thought of their work as charity–doing *for* someone less fortunate, out of religious or humanitarian conviction. Middle class African Americans believed that, in helping the less fortunate, the entire race would be tangibly–socially and economically–elevated; this belief is exemplified by the motto of the National Association of Colored Women's Clubs, "Lifting as We Climb."

As a consequence, "black women claimed leadership in looking after their whole people more than did comparable whites" (Gordon, 1991, p. 586), and advocated for universal social welfare provisions that were less concerned than the prevailing efforts in the larger society to separate the "worthy" from the "unworthy." African American reformers emphasized education and health rather than relief, and viewed human services as ". . . legal entitlements, not so different from the right to vote or to ride the public transportation system" (Gordon, 1991, p. 586).

This universal focus on social welfare provisions, the geographic proximity of middle and low income African Americans (who were equally confined to "Black belt" ghettoes), and the chronological closeness of the Black middle class to poverty (many were one generation out of slavery or sharecropping) all served to reduce the distance between helper and helped in the African American community.

Social Protest

African American protest for equal rights and equal justice declined during the Progressive Era, as Jim Crow laws and practices burrowed more deeply into the social fabric, in part because African American leaders acknowledged the futility of their efforts in the face of a white majority population growing increasingly hostile to integration and equality, and in part because many leaders turned their energies toward building separate African American institutions and communities (Meier, 1970). During these years, the ideological debate between followers of Booker T. Washington and W.E.B. DuBois influenced social protest at the local level. Through the Progressive Era, Bookerites were far more numerous than

DuBoisians, and the Black women's clubs particularly turned increasingly to self-help, and away from protest, as the Progressive years wore on (Giddings, 1984).

Many African American community leaders nevertheless mounted a variety of efforts to further goals of racial justice and equality. A few of them were ardently integrationist. Harry C. Smith, editor of Cleveland's Black newspaper, the *Gazette,* organized a campaign in opposition to Jane Hunter's Phyllis Wheatley Home, along with all other Black self-help programs, believing they only aided and abetted Jim Crow segregation. Smith's "ideas were in accord with the older Reconstructionist traditions and aspirations" (Meier, 1970, p. 74) and he opposed segregation at all costs (Kusmer, 1978). Most supporters of protest tactics to confront issues of Black equality, however, like Ida B. Wells-Barnett, found black self-help and protest goals mutually compatible.

Trying to arrest the rapid passage of Jim Crow laws during the Progressive Era was one important local protest issue. Between the years of 1900 and 1906, African American boycotts of city streetcars were mounted in at least 25 southern cities in response to newly enacted laws requiring segregation of public transportation facilities (Meier & Rudwick, 1968). In Louisville, the local NAACP branch got the courts to overturn a municipal segregation ordinance, mounting an ambitious public education campaign in the process to raise funds from the Black community to cover court costs (Rice, 1968). Atlanta Pastor Hugh Proctor successfully organized opposition to a bill that would have disfranchised African Americans (Lukar, 1984). In the North, Chicago Black community leaders organized to forestall efforts of the school board to re-segregate the schools (Spear, 1967), and Cleveland publisher Smith and two Ohio Black legislators led the fight to secure passage of the Civil Rights Act of 1886, forbidding segregation of public facilities (Meier, 1970).

The criminal justice system was of special concern to African American community activists because Blacks so blatantly received harsh and unfair treatment at the hands of the police, courts, and prisons (Gordon, 1991). Several women's groups organized campaigns to advocate for public programs for juvenile offenders (DuBois, 1909). The Negro Civic League of Kansas City sponsored a program called the Brotherhood (which also provided direct probation services) that collected data on irregularities in the dispensation of justice to Blacks in order to gain them pardons, and fought disorderly houses and illicit practices in the Black community (DuBois, 1909). To protest police brutality, 3500 Black New Yorkers met at Carnegie Hall in September 1900 to organize the Citizens' Protective League (Goldstein, 1977). The anti-lynching crusade was obviously yet another example of organized protest for a more equitable justice system, and one issue in which many African American women's clubs became actively involved.

The impulse that fueled the establishment of homes to protect working girls also led to reform efforts. A Black woman, S. Willie Layton, teamed with the better-known Frances Kellor in creating the National League for the Protection of Colored Women. They established the League after they used data from a fact-finding study of unscrupulous practices of employment agencies in New York to lobby for city licensing of employment bureaus and also for the first state-run employment agency (Osofsky, 1971). The League dispensed information through African American churches and institutions nationwide to alert women to unscrupulous operators (who would lure Black women into houses of prostitution), and it teamed with White Rose Mission workers in reaching out to migrating women when they arrived in major Northern cities.

IMPLICATIONS FOR COMMUNITY PRACTICE

This collective activity by and on behalf of African Americans in the Progressive years offers some lessons for present day community workers.

First, our forebears have shown us that there is no necessary dichotomy between community action organizing and community development. Both were needed to build strong communities. "Social protest" was needed to assure a more equitable distribution of society's resources to African American individuals, families, and communities. "Social betterment" was also needed, to build human capital and to protect the community's most vulnerable members. The fragmentation of efforts so often found today among community human services providers, community development corporations, and community action organizations lies in sharp contrast to organizations like the Neighborhood Union, the White Rose Mission, and the Brotherhood, which were able to integrate and phase these two important approaches to community building.

Second, our forebears showed us the strengths and the limits of self-help. Their legacy can help us temper the debates between advocates for big government and those for no government intervention in urban communities. Self-help provided an ideology that clearly connected the strength of the entire community to the futures of the community's most vulnerable citizens. Few modern day community organizations so clearly view dependent children, persistently poor families, wayward youth, and old people as community assets—too often recently these groups have been viewed as passive "clients." The self-help ideology itself fueled community building, through fundraising drives, health and public education campaigns that appealed to community pride, and the mobilization of neighbors for community research and social protest. At the same time, African American self-help was severely limited by lack of funds, and few programs survived for long. Our forebears' experience suggests that even relatively modest efforts relying heavily on volunteerism require philanthropic or public support to sustain their efforts.

Further, self-help was led by middle and upper income community members; the rag picker on the Negro Fellowship League's Board seems to have been exceptional. The Neighborhood Union's Board of Directors was of the middle income "directors," not the resident "presidents." By modern day standards, our Progessive forebears largely failed to develop lower income people for positions in community leadership. To some extent, this was the product of enormous class consciousness in the African American community in the Progressive Era. But to some extent, this experience portended the difficulties present-day organizing encounters in attempting to make community leaders of people struggling with day-to-day survival issues. Whatever the causes, the historical evidence suggests that the success of African American self-help was inextricably tied to the presence of middle income people in the black community, posing sobering implications for organizers in modern urban neighborhoods increasingly concentrated by class.

Thirdly, these African American community activists employed some community building methods that have great significance for re-developing African American and low-income communities today. Some of these methods have been incorporated into modern models of community practice; others seem to have been lost or misplaced. Among the methods that deserve serious reconsideration are:

- Lugenia Burns Hope organized highly systematic door-to-door campaigns conducted by neighborhood residents to build neighborliness and to identify at-risk families, a strategy now being re-considered by prevention specialists.
- Ida B. Wells-Barnett's Negro Fellowship League is an excellent example of "base community" organizing, or efforts to raise the political consciousness of small groups (Hanna & Robinson, 1994; McDougall, 1993). Modern day interest in base community organizing emanates from the liberation theologians in Central America; Wells-Barnett shows us how readily adaptable it is to the African American church.
- African American activists made extensive use of pre-existing community institutions–largely, schools and churches–as centers for comprehensive community building activities, in contrast to the strategy of creating new community organizations or settlement houses. This spirit is being rekindled today in the "beacon" schools movement and in some congregation-based organizing.
- Our African American forebears developed highly organized mechanisms of economic cooperation, to overcome capital shortages and "redlining" practices and to foster community cohesion. Such small-scale economic development ideas–micro business development, food and insurance and housing cooperatives–are a necessity in the post-Great Society era. But they are also being instituted explicitly as one important means of creating community (McDougall, 1993; Leiterman & Stillman, 1993).
- The Progressive African American community was highly sophisticated in its use of available media. Journalists were prominent activists, and the local press was a powerful tool in assuring successful protests and public education. The pulpit

was a significant force in this media strategy, reaching vast numbers of people who were illiterate. With the mass media revolution, organizers today may overlook the power of the local press and pulpit.

Fourthly, our African American forebears in community building benefitted greatly from being actively involved with nationwide networks of community activists. The National Association of Colored Women's Clubs was a phenomenally successful tool in getting model programs, like homes for working girls, replicated throughout the country. The Association was also an effective vehicle in its early days in getting protest issues placed on local clubs' agendas. Associations of Black editors, churches, businesses, and men's clubs also helped connect local activists with one another. The national associations equally benefitted, by having their issues legitimated and lobbied by local community organizations. Martin Kilson (1971) has noted the importance of two national organizations–the NAACP and the Urban League–in "the integration into the national political arena of Negro urban voluntary associations (churches, mutual benefit societies, economic cooperatives) . . ." (p. 367).

Finally, one cannot help but be inspired by the skill, the dignity, the energy, and the persistence of these activists–and especially the women–who pressed on under incredible adversity. Racism, sexism, persistent poverty, and blatant injustice permeated the lives of African American community activists. They, and their work, were derided or ignored by the press and by most of their White peers. It is time for us to remember their struggles, honor their heroism, learn from their experiences, and incorporate their thought and action into "mainstream" community work history.

BIBLIOGRAPHIC NOTE

This note seeks to guide social workers, other community practitioners, and social work students through the historical literature.

For general reading on *African American history,* begin with J.H. Franklin (1980). For general reading on the *African American heritage in community development,* begin with Ross (1978) and Kusmer, vol. 1 (1991).

For reading on *African American community development before the Progres-*

sive Era, see J.H. Franklin (1980), V.P. Franklin (1992), Meier and Rudwick (1970), Litwack and Meier (1988), and Scott (1990).

Hofstadter (1981) and Mann (1975) are excellent sources on *the Progressive Era.* On the *African-American urban migration,* see J.H. Franklin (1980), Grossman (1985), Haynes (1913), Meier and Rudwick (1970), and Meier (1970). The impact of the migration on individual cities is described in Connolly (1977), Kusmer (1978), Osofsky (1971), and Spear (1967). Also, reprints of articles describing the growth of black communities in Buffalo, Detroit, Columbus, San Francisco, Seattle, and others are found in volumes 4 and 5 of Kusmer (1991). On *the growing segregation in the Progressive Era,* in addition to the sources on the migration, see Fredrickson (1971), Kusmer (1986), Weinstein and Gettell (1970), and Woodward (1974).

On the *ideological debate* among the accomodationists, integrationists, and nationalists, see Meier (1970), V.P. Franklin (1992), and Lewis (1993).

For reading on *Progressive Era black community development efforts,* see DuBois (1909), Jackson (1978), Pollard (1978), and volume 4 of Kusmer (1991). See also Connolly (1977), Jackson (1978), Kusmer (1978), Osofsky (1971), and Spear (1967) for discussions of community development in individual cities.

REFERENCES

Addams, J. (1961). *Twenty years at Hull-House.* New York: Signet Classics.

Betten, N. & Austin, M. J. (1990). *The roots of community organizing, 1917-1939.* Philadelphia: Temple University Press.

Burghardt, S. (1987). Community-based social action. In the National Association of Social Workers, *Encyclopedia of Social Work,* 18th ed. (pp. 292-293). Silver Spring, MD: NASW Press.

Connolly, H. X. (1977). *A ghetto grows in Brooklyn.* New York: New York University.

DuBois, W. E. B. (1909). *Efforts for social betterment among Negro Americans.* Atlanta University Publications No. 14. Atlanta: Atlanta University Press.

Duster, A. M. (Ed.) (1970). *Crusade for justice: The autobiography of Ida B. Wells.* Chicago: The University of Chicago Press.

Fisher, R. & Romanofsky, P. (1981). *Community organization for urban social change: A historical perspective.* (pp. xi-xviii.) Westport, CT: Greenwood Press.

Franklin, J. H. (1980). *From slavery to freedom: A history of Negro Americans,* 5th ed. New York: Alfred A. Knopf.

Franklin, V. P. (1992). *Black self-determination: A cultural history of African American resistance,* 2nd rev. ed. Brooklyn: L. Hill.

Fredrickson, G. M. (1971). *The Black image in the white mind: The debate on Afro-American character and destiny, 1817-1914.* New York: Harper & Row.

Giddings, P. (1984). *When and where I enter: The impact of Black women on race and sex in America.* New York: William Morrow.

Goldstein, M. L. (1977). Preface to the rise of Booker T. Washington: A view from New York City of the demise of independent black politics, 1889-1902. *Journal of Negro History,* 62(1), 81-99. Reprinted in Kusmer, K. (Ed.) (1991). *Black communities and urban development in America, vol. 4, no. 2,* (pp. 229-232). New York: Garland Publishing.

Gordon, L. (1991). Black and white visions of welfare: Women's welfare activism, 1890-1945. *The Journal of American History,* 78(September), 559-589.

Grossman, J. R. (1985). Blowing the trumpet: The *Chicago Defender* and Black migration during World War I. *Illinois Historical Journal,* 78(2), 82-96. Reprinted in Kusmer, K. (Ed.) (1991). *Black communities and urban development in America, vol 5.* (pp. 2-4). New York: Garland Publishing.

Hanna, M. G. & Robinson, B. (1994). *Strategies for community Empowerment: Direct-action and transformative approaches to social change practice.* Lewiston, NY: The Edwin Mellen Press.

Haynes, G. E. (1913). Conditions among Negroes in cities. *Annals of the American Academy of Political and Social Science, 49,* 105-19. Reprinted in K. Kusmer (Ed.) (1991) *Black communities and Urban development in America, 1790-1920, vol. 4, no. 2.* (p. 14). New York: Garland Publishing.

Hofstadter, R. (1981). *The age of reform: from Bryan to F.D.R.* New York: Alfred A. Knopf.

Jackson, P. (1978). Black charity in Progressive Era Chicago. *Social Service Review 52*(September), 400-417.

Kilson, M. (1971). Political change in the Negro ghetto, 1900-1940's. In N. Huggins et. al. (Eds.) (1971). *Key issues in the Afro-American experience.* New York: Harcourt Brace Jovanovich. Reprinted in K. Kusmer (Ed.) (1991). *Black communities and urban development,* vol. 5. (p. 367). New York: Garland Publishing.

Kramer, R. M. and Specht, H. (1975). *Readings in community organization practice.* Englewood Cliffs, NJ: Prentice-Hall, pp. 9-10.

Kusmer, K. (1978). *A ghetto takes shape: Black Cleveland, 1870-1930.* Urbana: University of Illinois Press.

Kusmer, K. (1986). The Black urban experience in American history. In D.C. Hine (Ed.) (1986). *The state of Afro-American history: past, present, and future.* Baton Rouge: LSU Press. Reprinted in K. Kusmer (Ed.) (1991). *Black communities and urban development, vol. 9.* (pp.33-64). New York: Garland Publishing.

Kusmer, K., ed. (1991). *Black communities and urban development in America, 1790-1920,* vols.1-10. New York: Garland Publishing.

Leiterman, M. & Stillman, J. (1993). *Building community.* New York: Local Initiatives Support Corporation.

Lerner, G. (1974). Early community work of Black club women. *Journal of Negro History, 59*(April), 158-167.

Lewis, D. L. (1993). *W.E.B. DuBois: Biography of a race 1868-1919.* New York: Henry Holt.

Litwack, L. & Meier, A. (Eds.) (1988). *Black leaders of the nineteenth century.* Urbana: University of Illinois Press.

Lukar, R. E. (1984). Missions, institutional churches, and settlement houses: The Black experience, 1885-1910, *Journal of Negro History, 69*(Summer/Fall), 101-113.

Mann, A. ed. (1975). *The Progressive Era: Major issues of interpretation,* 2nd ed. Hinsdale, IL: Dryden Press.

McDougall, H. A. (1993). *Black Baltimore: A new theory of community.* Philadelphia: Temple University Press.

Meier, A. (1970). *Negro thought in America 1890-1915.* Ann Arbor MI: Ann Arbor Paperbacks.

Meier, A. & Rudwick, E. (1970). *From plantation to ghetto,* rev.ed. New York: Hill and Wang.

Meier, A. & Rudwick, E. (1968). The boycott movement against Jim Crow streetcars in the South, 1900-1906. *Journal of American History, 55*(4), 756-75. Reprinted in K. Kusmer (Ed.) (1991). *Black communities and urban development, vol. 4, part 1.* (pp. 268-287). New York: Garland Publishing.

Osofsky, G. (1971). *Harlem: The making of a ghetto, Negro New York, 1890-1930,* 2nd ed. New York: Harper and Row.

Peebles-Wilkins, W. & Francis, E. A. (1990). Two outstanding black women in social welfare history: Mary Church Terrell and Ida B. Wells-Barnett, *Affilia, 5*(Winter), 87-100.

Pollard, W. P. (1978). *A study of Black self-help.* San Francisco: R&E Research Associates.

Rice, R. L. (1968). Residential segregation by law, 1910-1917, *Journal of Southern History, 43*(2), 179-199.

Ross, E. L. (1978). *Black heritage in social welfare 1860-1930.* Metuchen, NJ: Scarecrow Press.

Rothman, J. & Tropman, J. E. (1987). Models of community organization and macro practice perspectives: Their mixing and phasing. In F.M. Cox et al. (Eds.) (1987). *Strategies of community organization,* 4th ed. (pp. 3-26). Itasca, IL: Peacock.

Rouse, J. A. (1984). The legacy of community organizing: Lugenia Burns Hope and the Neighborhood Union, *Journal of Negro History, 69*(Summer/Fall), 114-133.

Rouse, J. A. (1989). *Lugenia Burns Hope: Black southern reformer.* Athens, GA: University of Georgia Press.

Scott, A. F. (1990). Most invisible of all: Black women's voluntary associations, *Journal of Southern History, 56*(February), 3-22.

Shivery, L. D. (1936). The history of organized social work among Atlanta Negroes, 1980-1935. Master's Thesis: Atlanta University. Reprinted in E.L. Ross (Ed.) (1978). *Black heritage in social welfare 1860-1930* (pp. 264-268). Metuchen, NJ: Scarecrow Press.

Spear, A. (1967). *Black Chicago: The making of a Negro ghetto, 1890-1920.* Chicago: University of Chicago Press.

Spergel, I. (1987). Community development. In National Association of Social

Workers (Eds.) (1987). *Encyclopedia of Social Work, 18th ed., vol.1.* (p. 300). Silver Spring, MD: NASW Press.

Tuttle, W., Jr. (1977). *Race riot: Chicago in the Red Summer of 1919.* New York: Atheneum.

Weil, M. O. & Gamble, G. (1995). Community practice models. In National Association of Social Workers, *Encyclopedia of Social Work, 19th ed.* (pp. 577-594). Washington, D.C.: NASW Press.

Weinstein, A. & Gettell, F.O. (1970). *The segregation era 1863-1954: A modern reader.* New York: Oxford University Press.

Williams, F. B. (1905). Social bonds in the 'black belt' of Chicago. *Charities, 15* (October 7), 40-43.

Woodward, C.V. (1974). *The strange career of Jim Crow, 3rd ed.* New York: Oxford University Press.

George and Birdye Haynes' Legacy to Community Practice

Iris Carlton-LaNey, PhD

SUMMARY. This paper looks at the careers of George Edmund Haynes and his younger sister Birdye Henrietta Haynes and their legacy to community practice. Both of the Hayneses were professionally trained social workers and graduates from two pioneer schools of social work, George from the New York School of Philanthropy and Birdye from the Chicago School of Civics and Philanthropy. They each made significant contributions to the development of the profession and to community practice in the African American community. This paper highlights several of their professional experiences with a focus on their "race work," and discusses the community practice strategies and approaches that they used. *[Article copies available from The Haworth Document Delivery Service: 1-800-342-9678.]*

KEYWORDS. African American, community practice, Black social work, race work, social welfare

The Progressive Era, between 1900 and World War I, was a period of tremendous social and economic change in the United

Iris Carlton-LaNey is Associate Professor of Social Work at the University of North Carolina at Chapel Hill.

Address correspondence to: Dr. Iris Carlton-LaNey, School of Social Work, CB#3550, University of North Carolina at Chapel Hill, Chapel Hill, NC 27599-3550.

[Haworth co-indexing entry note]: "George and Birdye Haynes' Legacy to Community Practice." Carlton-LaNey, Iris. Co-published simultaneously in *Journal of Community Practice* (The Haworth Press, Inc.) Vol. 2, No. 4, 1995, pp. 27-48; and: *African American Community Practice Models: Historical and Contemporary Responses* (ed: Iris Carlton-LaNey, and N. Yolanda Burwell) The Haworth Press, Inc., 1996, pp. 27-48. Single or multiple copies of this article are available from The Haworth Document Delivery Service [1-800-342-9678, 9:00 a.m. - 5:00 p.m. (EST)].

27

States. For many White Americans, the basic conditions of life significantly improved with advances in technology, increased citizen participation and governmental responsiveness, and new social legislation that included antitrust laws, child labor laws, and health and safety laws (Day, 1989). For many African Americans, however, the Progressive Era did not bring such positive change. Rather, during that time period, African Americans experienced increased economic and social hardships, exclusion from labor markets, and increased segregation and discriminatory governmental legislation. Essentially the Progressive Era represented what one expert describes as one "of the ironies of American history that what is ordinarily characterized as a period of democratic upsurge or reform has in fact meant something else for the Negro" (Kogut, 1970, p. 11).

For African Americans, the Progressive Era marked the elevation of problematic welfare situations from local to national proportions as over a million African Americans moved into urban centers largely from the rural south. Both economic and social causes produced this migration. In the economic sphere, the ravages of the cotton boll weevil, unusual floods, the growth of commercial and industrial centers, the shortage of labor in the North, and the divorce of African Americans from the soil, all dramatically affected the material basis of the lives of Southern African Americans. Social developments included Jim Crowism, lynching, peonage, poor housing, and the generally neglected environment of African American sections of towns. Exaggerated stories of success in the Northern cities, along with the promises from labor agents of jobs and the lure of free railroad tickets to the North also served as a prime impetus for migration (Fulks, 1969, p. 220; Ross, 1978, p. 284; DuBois, 1912, pp. 641-42).

To confound the situation further, the masses of African Americans leaving rural areas were not prepared to meet the exacting requirements of organized industry in cities, nor were they given the access to opportunities that European immigrants enjoyed. African Americans were shut out of organized labor because of their lack of skill and similarly excluded from unorganized labor because they represented competitors who could be eliminated on the basis of race (Kogut, 1970). Further, the Woodrow Wilson administration demonstrated a similar trend toward the exclusion of African Americans. Within a few months after his inauguration, it became evident that a color line was being established within the departments of the federal government. In addition, Southern Democrats dominated Wilson's cabinet and controlled many important congressional committees and caucuses in both Houses. Unofficial segregation and the concurrent rise of Southern seniority in the Congress were subsequently followed by the largest amount of anti-African American legislation ever before proposed in a United States Congress. These events had both symbolic and practical overtones, for they succeeded in setting national precedents for segregation and discrimination which spread to the rest of the country (Fulks, 1969).

African American "self-help" emerged, in part, because of the group's overwhelming exclusion from full participation in the American social system, because of the limited response of White social workers to the individual and social problems of African Americans in the early twentieth century, and out of a desire to take care of their own. By necessity, welfare practices designed to attack, in an organized way, the many social problems affecting these rapidly growing African American communities were developed within the African American community itself. The challenge of improving the living and working conditions of African Americans coupled with intensified segregation, repression, and discrimination fostered several organized efforts and encouraged many individuals to step forward and engage in the struggle to develop services and programs which would ensure a higher quality of life for people of African American ancestry.

As community leaders and organizers emerged during the Progressive Era, George Edmund Haynes and his sister Birdye Henrietta Haynes took their place as prominent pioneer advocates and crusaders of social justice. Their work was a strategic response to the myriad social problems and individual hardships that confronted the African American community. In general, their contributions as professionally trained social workers have been excluded from the social work literature. This gives a skewed picture of the history of social work and social welfare and leaves one to conclude that African Americans contributed very little to the organization and development of the social work profession. As this article demonstrates, this is not the case. The Haynes' careers made an impact on social welfare at the national, regional, and local levels. Their work influenced the development of both macro and micro level social work, contributing not only to the social work methods of practice, but to the development of social welfare organizations as well. The web of racism pervasive during the Progressive Era complicated their tasks and has contributed to their relative obscurity in social work history. Nonetheless, their accomplishments deserve a place in that history and we can learn from their work. The essay below documents the importance of the Haynes' contributions to social work history and provides valuable information from which the profession of social work and the method of community practice can benefit.

BRIEF HISTORY OF GEORGE AND BIRDYE HAYNES

George Edmund Haynes and his younger sister Birdye Henrietta Haynes began to embrace the tenets of community practice very early in their professional careers. Born in Pine Bluff, Arkansas, the Haynes children grew up in a very strict religious home and learned the ideals of Christian fellowship from their mother who was a furiously religious woman. Their mother encouraged her children to care about the well-being of others as part of their Christian obligation. She set high goals for her children with an intent to provide them with opportunities that were not generally available to the African American youth of the day. The values and social obligations that the Haynes children embraced were reenforced at Fisk University in Nashville, Tennessee, where both George and Birdye Haynes matriculated and graduated—George in 1903 and Birdye in 1911. Their education at Fisk University included the spirit of voluntarism as well as a commitment to community involvement and planned change. The strong race antagonism of the Progressive Era that denied African Americans access to opportunities, threatened their health and safety, and preyed on their economic and political vulnerability, influenced George and Birdye Haynes' decisions about their personal and professional responsibilities. The Haynes' pride in being African Americans and the price that they were forced to pay for that existence encouraged them to engage in the struggle for social justice and equity. Each of these elements combined to provide a lasting shape to the course of their careers.

Education and Commitment

Both George and Birdye Haynes were professionally trained social workers. George was the first African American to graduate from the New York School of Philanthropy in 1910 (Carlton-LaNey, 1983), and Birdye was the first African American to graduate from the Chicago School of Civics and Philanthropy in 1914 (Carlton-LaNey, 1994b). By 1912, George Haynes had also earned a doctorate degree in sociology and economics from Columbia University. As educated African Americans, much was expected of them. They were among the "talented tenth," the educated leaders of the African American community (DuBois, 1903), and they worked zealously accepting the role of "race man" and "race woman." As members of the African American intelligentsia, George and Birdye Haynes recognized that their roles were pivotal in tackling the problems that confronted all African Americans. As George Haynes stated in 1936, "College and university men and women carried with them the obligation of their opportunity so to serve the people . . . as to lead them out of the wilderness of war and poverty and race prejudice . . ." (Private papers in Mt. Vernon, NY).

The terms "race man" and "race woman" were used in 1945 by Drake and Cayton in their book, *Black Metropolis*. The "race man" was the individual who was reputed to be uncompromising in his fight to ensure African Americans equal access to opportunity. He was proud of his race and culture and he was engaged in activities to benefit his people. The race woman had many of the same qualities and engaged in the same activities as the race man but was believed to wield less influence among Whites than her male counterpart. Because she was less powerful in the larger community, the African American community regarded the race woman with less suspicion than they did the race man. The race woman understood the circumstances of her people and was likely to engage in studies of their social, economic, and political conditions. Her work was always to uplift the race and to teach appropriate, suitable, and necessary life skills (Drake & Cayton, 1962). Race work was essentially community advocacy coupled with the constant struggle for social justice and racial equality. Race work was such an integral part of George and Birdye Haynes' lives and careers that it formed the foundation upon which they worked and served to endear them to their people. Both of the Hayneses were accepted by African Americans as sincere race workers and as leaders because they were humble enough to relate to and identify with the working class community, yet educated and articulate enough to be respected by the "Black bourgeoisie" and to a lesser extent the White establishment.

THE WORK OF GEORGE HAYNES

George Haynes had a strong and far-reaching social work career. He can be credited with helping to establish and develop many social work services and programs. That he was co-founder and first executive director of the National Urban League (NUL) is his most significant and enduring contribution to the profession of social work. The NUL, founded in 1911, had become synonymous with social work in the African American community by 1916. Through the NUL, George Haynes worked to provide skilled social work services to the population of African Americans migrating from the rural south to urban centers in the north. The NUL was a major social welfare movement comparable in influence and impact to the Charity Organization Society (COS) and the settlement house movement (Carlton-LaNey, 1994a). The NUL's mission was to attack the social problems that African Americans faced as they migrated from the rural south to urban centers in the North. The organization's goals included (1) demonstrating to social welfare agencies the advantages of cooperation, (2) securing and training social workers, (3) protecting women and children from unscrupulous persons, (4) fitting workers for/to work, (5) helping to secure playgrounds and other clean places of amusement, (6) organizing boys' and girls' clubs and neighborhood unions, (7) working with delinquents, (8) maintaining a country home for convalescent women, and (9) investigating conditions of city life as a basis for practical work (Carlton-LaNey, 1984; Parris & Brooks, 1971; Weiss, 1974). The NUL, like the settlement house movement, was the very hallmark of community practice with a sense of community solidarity forming the cornerstone of the organization. The reasons for the establishment of the NUL and the activities of that organization epitomized community practice and embraced the methods and processes of organizing, planning, development, and change.

Interdependence, mutual aid, and a reality of shared experiences placed the NUL squarely within the daily existence of the urban African American community. The times dictated that any organization or movement designed to impact the African American community must be community based, community sensitive, and community valued in order to be worthwhile. While there were certainly class differences among African Americans, the White community's practice of physical and social segregation placed African Americans together within the same physical space. Unlike the leaders of the COS and to a lesser extent the settlement houses, NUL leaders traditionally lived and worked within the same communities in which they socialized and worshiped. The risk of devaluing others, out of ignorance of their lives and daily circumstances, was not a reality for leaders like George Haynes. He was sensitive to these issues and emphasized the importance of shared community values. He felt that people who best understood the conditions that affect the lives of African American people must live with them and "share with them the life of the Negro world." "Only Negroes live with that world," Haynes (1920) noted.

With this understanding, George Haynes set about the task of training African American social workers to deliver skilled social services to their communities. To ensure that these social workers were linked with the serious conditions that existed among African American urban dwellers, he established the Department of Social Sciences at Fisk University in 1912. This program prepared students to enter the profession of social work and included courses in economics, sociology, social work, and African American history. Students enrolled in the social work program at Fisk could expect to become very familiar with the community surrounding the university. Historically, African American colleges and universities have been criticized for being too elitist. On the other hand, Jones (1971) contends that these schools were charged with developing a cadre of people who could challenge and overcome immediate threats to the survival of the African American community while working simultaneously for equal status in American society. He asserts that these schools collectively met their responsibilities. It was therefore not unusual for students enrolled in African American colleges and universities to be intimately involved with the community. Haynes believed that it was essential that students who expected to make a positive impact on their communities be given all of the tools necessary for helping to make the community strong. He required seniors in the Social Sciences Program to work in the community for four hours per week for a thirty-week period and to spend six additional hours in the study of methods of statistics and social investigation, totaling ten hours per week for all field involvement (Fisk University Bulletin, 1913, p. 48). Students enrolled in the social problems classes were required to go in pairs to visit some of the neglected and blighted districts of Nashville in order to develop a better understanding of conditions and life quality.

The Fisk social work students' mandatory integration into the local Nashville community in their volunteer work helped them to understand their neighbors' problems and concerns. These students' professional mission, according to Haynes, was ". . . to be vitally articulated with the conditions and needs of the Negroes in the communities" in which their college was located (Haynes, 1911, p. 385). In addition to field work, each student was required to live and work at Bethlehem Center which was a local social settlement house. The Fisk social work students staffed the Center which involved planning, implementing, and supervising the settlement house activities. The array of activities at Bethlehem Center included working with Camp Fire Girls groups, teaching courses in domestic science and sewing, maintaining a kindergarten, and working with men's cooperative clubs and junior and intermediate boys' clubs (Bulletin of the NLUCAN, 1915, p. 29).

The East Nashville Fire of 1916: Relief Work and Student Involvement

The relief work undertaken by George Haynes and his students during and after the East Nashville Fire of March 22, 1916 provides an excellent example of Haynes' commitment to training students to work effectively in the community. The fire destroyed the homes of 324 African Americans and 301 White families who lived near the Fisk University campus. George Haynes and the social work students enrolled at Fisk University played a significant role in providing relief to the families who were victims of the fire. The social work students' relief work carried the message of community concern and involvement and indicated their commitment to social betterment. These students and local community leaders assumed leadership during the disaster, assessing need, coordinating community resources, and distributing resources to the fire victims.

George Haynes and the students responded to the disaster of the East Nashville fire even before it was brought under control. After Haynes and his assistant, Paul Mowbray, "walked out on Jefferson Street to the bridge and saw where the fire had been and the place where it was then burning," they began an informal survey "inquiring to the extent of suffering and loss of residents." Responding to a call from a local community leader, Haynes attended a meeting later that evening ". . . to see what could be done for the fire sufferers" (Haynes, nd).

As a result of the meeting, George Haynes and the social work students were to organize some form of assistance for the fire victims. The students were divided into two groups of field staff and office staff. Haynes supervised the office staff of students and Mowbray, who had experience in relief work in New York City, supervised the students who were part of the field staff. Haynes maintained meticulous records of the relief work of which the students were a part. He felt that it was essential to keep cogent records (1) as a way to inform contributors of ways that their monies were used, (2) as a mechanism to dissuade criticism and controversies, and (3) as a way to provide a guide for future emergencies (Haynes, nd).

The community survey research in which the Fisk students participated gave them a strong foundation for their relief work. Edward Devine's book *Principles of Relief and Misery and Its Causes and Efficiency and Relief,* which presented the relief efforts that took place following the Chicago Fire, the Johnstown Flood, and several other serious disasters, was also essential in helping the students to understand the various problems associated with disasters. Their social problems classes had prepared them with analytical skills, and their intimate involvement with the community had helped to familiarize them with the social networks, lifestyles, and values of the Nashville community. With a thorough grounding in research and a familiarity with the customs and traditions of the community, the students' work was efficient and effective enough to garner the support of others. They were soon joined by students from the Agricultural and Industrial State Normal School, Meharry Medical College, and Roger Williams University of Nashville. The Fisk students' relief work was detailed and extensive. They developed an "emergency relief card" for each individual seeking service, surveyed household losses and the sizes, ages and conditions of members of each family, and made personal visits to the temporary addresses of all applicants to inspect their circumstances and to make first-hand assessments of their apparent needs (Carlton-LaNey, 1985; Haynes, nd).

The Negro Board of Trade and the Commercial Club, a White business organization in Nashville, worked with Haynes, Mowbray, and the college students from the various schools in the city. The domestic science experts from Fisk University also joined forces with this group to give instruction to the fire victims regarding the art of economically preparing and serving food. The relief work was clearly a community effort; and George Haynes' skills as an organizer were apparent. He knew when to ask for help and when to share responsibilities. He also easily shared his expertise and that of the students with the community. Rivera and Erlich (1992) indicate that these are essential qualities of a skilled organizer. Months after the relief work ended, the secretary of the Commercial Club wrote to Haynes in appreciation for his "very efficient work" during the disaster and credited him with the success of the relief work.

THE WORK OF BIRDYE HAYNES

Like her brother, Birdye Haynes was also intimately concerned with the improvement and development of local urban communities. Her work as a settlement house worker in Chicago at the Wendell Phillips Settlement and later at New York's Lincoln House clearly illustrates the extent of her understanding and involvement in community practice (Carlton-LaNey, 1994b). While Birdye Haynes may not have been as influential in the development of the social work profession as her more famous brother, she nonetheless made significant contributions to the profession, to the community, and to the lives of individuals touched by her work at the two major social settlements established to serve the African American community.

As a graduate of the Chicago School of Civics and Philanthropy, Birdye Haynes' social work education emphasized both cause and function. The school's leaders believed that social work should be both an academic discipline as well as a profession and that social change and individual treatment were both essential. With a substantial grant from the Laura Spelman Rockefeller Foundation, the Chicago School escaped dominance by the practice community and moved to develop an academic macro practice approach to social work (Popple, 1978). The macro focus of Birdye Haynes' training at the Chicago School, the Fisk University orientation of "social debt," and the "talented tenth" obligation for educated African Americans to be "leaders of thought and missionaries of culture among their people" (DuBois, 1903, p. 48), formed the doctrine that guided her work in the social settlements. Birdye Haynes' settlement house work involved advocacy, community development and planning, and service development and delivery. She was constantly advocating for the welfare of the community residents, for more meaningful social work services, and for better-trained social workers to provide those services.

Settlement House Work in New York City

Birdye Haynes spent the years 1915-1922 as Administrator of New York's Lincoln House Settlement. The Lincoln House Settlement was founded by the leaders of the Henry Street Settlement to serve New York's African American community. Like most social settlements, strict segregation practices existed at the Henry Street Settlement. Rather than serve African Americans, the Henry Street leadership established Lincoln House to meet the needs of the African American community. Lincoln House provided services such as mothers' clubs, educational classes, and recreational activities to community members.

Birdye Haynes was a gifted and strong administrator at Lincoln House Settlement. Professionally trained and experienced in settlement house work, Birdye was skillful in program planning and development and in administration. She had a strong sense of self and was aware of her strengths and of the limits of her position as settlement house matron; and she was committed to the growth and development of the African American community. Birdye Haynes' brother, in later years, described her administration as one that embraced ". . . developments in improving neighborhood living" (Carlton-LaNey, 1994b).

Birdye took her administrative duties very seriously and respected the role of the board that governed New York's Lincoln House Settlement. She had learned a great deal from her work at Chicago's Wendell Phillips Settlement, which also served the African American community, including the dangers of a weak and detached board (Carlton-LaNey, 1994b). She trusted her experience to guide her work in New York, and she knew that in order for her work to be successful, she needed a strong board that shared her commitment and passion. Birdye Haynes' insight indicates her understanding of community practice. In direct service agencies, like Lincoln House, the administrator's relationship with the governing board is of paramount significance in mobilizing community support. The board-executive relationship is ideally a partnership in which both have equal status (Kramer, 1969). Birdye Haynes knew that the existing sociopolitical structure which devalued African Americans would make the development of an equal partnership between administrator and board a difficult task, at best. She did, nonetheless, accept the fact that the board-executive relationship was pivotal if her work at Lincoln House was to succeed.

The Lincoln House 15-member board was very well organized and operated under the auspices of the Henry Street Settlement. The board included prominent men and women, both African American and White, who worked with major social welfare organizations throughout the city. In an effort to determine the strength of the board, aspects of the board members' status and level of identification with the settlement house, Birdye made numerous inquiries about specific members and about the board in general. Birdye knew that mobilizing community support depended on an array of strategies not the least of which included prominent board support, shared values and similar perceptions of the settlement's role in the African American community (Carlton-LaNey, 1994b). She also knew that she had to exercise caution in her work with the board. Her role was complicated by both her race and gender. There were strict codes of behavior for African American women to which Birdye Haynes had to adhere. In this environment, she was required to be diplomatic, tactful, and reticent as she interacted with the professionals, educators, advisory boards and community residents who were all key players in the success or failure of the house.

As Birdye sought leave from Wendell Phillips Settlement to interview in New York, she discussed the perspective position at Lincoln House with her mentor, Edith Abbott, a settlement house pioneer and professor at the Chicago School of Civics and Philanthropy. Abbott said that she was familiar with the Henry Street Settlement, of which Lincoln House was a branch, and suggested to Birdye that she get as much out of her New York trip as possible. To that end, Abbott encouraged Birdye to meet with some of George Haynes' friends and colleagues while in New York including Ruth Baldwin, co-founder of the NUL (Birdye Haynes to George Haynes, 1915a). Abbott's suggestions to the younger Haynes echoed the salient role of gathering support by establishing linkages with individuals and organizations who were influential in the community's social and political life (Siedner, 1969). Abbott also reassured Birdye that she was eminently qualified for the position at Lincoln House and ". . . would be nicely entertained there" (Birdye Haynes to George Haynes, 1915a).

Birdye Haynes also communicated frequently with her brother and his wife, Elizabeth, about specific board members, living arrangements, and hiring decisions. With what she felt was "good advice" (Birdye Haynes to George Haynes, 1915a) received from her brother, Birdye concluded that she would be willing to accept the position as matron at Lincoln House, "if the work has any kind of Board that will stand responsible for a passable salary and support in the work" (Birdye Haynes to George Haynes, 1915b). Upon her visit to New York, Birdye spent "four very busy days . . . studying the neighborhood about Lincoln House, and seeing other work among colored people" (Birdye Haynes to George Haynes, 1915c). She also met the staff at the headquarters of the NUL and found that Eugene Jones, the Field Secretary for the organization, was very helpful. Jones was also a Lincoln House board member, which further reas-

sured her. Birdye Haynes was heartened by her meeting with the
Lincoln House board. She felt that they were warm, sincere and
committed to the work of the house. She was encouraged when at the
conclusion of her meeting with three of the board members, they
formally offered her the position and "each took my hand and
pledged her support" (Birdye Haynes to George Haynes, 1915c).

As Birdye interacted with her board in later months, she was
careful to present well prepared, thorough, and detailed reports. She
sought board approval for any changes that she wished to make in
the house; and she was skilled in using her board to the best advantage of the settlement house and of the community. She recognized
the personal and political power of her board members and solicited
their help with both personnel and programmatic issues.

Birdye also understood the institutional barriers that interfered
with her role as matron. She was sometimes frustrated by the politics of racism, but never deterred by the restraints that these barriers
of racial segregation and political disfranchisement placed on her
and the success of activities at the house. As a newcomer to New
York, Birdye Haynes was concerned that she might be at a disad-
vantage in working with the neighborhood residents. She spent
considerable time making decisions that would facilitate her work
and best serve the community and its residents. Hiring an assistant
was Birdye's first major personnel task as head matron. As she
began the process, she questioned ". . . the idea of selecting a home
or N.Y. girl because of the possibility of lack of full cooperation and
sympathy with me which is so necessary if we together are to do the
most effective work." Birdye believed that a New York native,
"being in her own field, would give her an advantage over me and
she may later resent 'being under me'" (Birdye Haynes to George
Haynes, 1915c). Birdye and George, after consulting with Jones,
concluded that the selection of a New York woman would best
serve all involved. Jones suggested that it would be very difficult to
engage the New York community if both the head worker and her
assistant were "new comers" (George Haynes to Birdye Haynes,
1915b). Jones also reassured George Haynes that he would not
allow anyone to sabotage Birdye's work. Assured of the board
support and of an ally in Jones, Birdye embraced the role as head
matron with determination.

As an advocate for the welfare of the community residents, Birdye knew that her close contact with the community was necessary for useful social work to take place and she constantly worked to develop a strong relationship with local residents. She also examined the needs of the community closely and developed programs to meet their needs. The settlement's programs included numerous clubs and classes, such as the City History Club, the Lincoln House Girl Scouts, the Stillman Mother's Club, and the dramatic club. The house included a gymnasium which was usually occupied by boys' games of basketball, boxing and pool. A kindergarten and a roof garden rounded out the settlement's activities. Wholesome recreation and constructive use of leisure time were priorities in Birdye Haynes' programming. At the conclusion of a summer of intense activities of field trips, community gardening, fresh air camping, and street parties, Haynes reported that "we have lived together in this outdoor life all during the long hot summer and we feel that we know and understand each other better and can better help and comfort one another during the days that lie before us" (Haynes, 1916-17).

Birdye Haynes was committed to the community in which the settlement was located. While she was from a rural background and part of the educated elite, she was, nonetheless, a part of the community's culture and identified closely with them. Her door was always open to community residents. On most evenings the house did not close until well after 10:00 p.m. Birdye attended club meetings and parties of various groups meeting at the settlement. She worshiped in the local community, helped families in crisis, helped newcomers to find employment, and attended funerals when local residents died. As Rivera and Erlich (1992) point out, community leaders must recognize cultural gaps and work to close them where they exist. Birdye Haynes mastered this skill and more, and was very well-liked and respected in the community in which she worked.

It should be noted that part of a conscious plan to fight racism among African American women included teaching members of their race to appear and behave in a way that would nullify and dispel stereotypes which identified them as dependent, uncivilized, and/or amoral (Lasch-Quinn, 1993). Birdye acknowledged that responsibility and wrote to her board in 1917 that her role involved "breaking down prejudices and misconceptions." Birdye did not presume to have all of the answers to problems that presented themselves and was receptive to others' ideas and input. She did, however, love the community and its residents which was a motivational factor in her leadership role as head worker of the settlement.

While Birdye Haynes engaged in many activities as Lincoln House matron, one incident in particular illustrates her skill and determination as a community advocate. The vignette below also demonstrates Birdye Haynes' skills in conscientization and empowerment. In her 1915 annual report to the Board, she wrote:

> There were 15 boys present (ages 14-15) who call themselves "the gang" and have been a nuisance about the House and neighborhood. Their energy runs up to the savage point; they are loyal to each other as Damon and Pythias and will fight the common foe like German soldiers. (Birdye Haynes, 1915)

Apparently, "the gang" was seen as a major problem at Lincoln House and in the Columbus Hill community. Many participants had encouraged Haynes to restrict "the gang" from participating in House activities. Birdye Haynes was determined that these children and all children in the neighborhood should have an opportunity to be involved in the activities at the settlement. As Franklin and Moss (1994) noted, juvenile delinquency was rampant in the growing slums of cities and there were few corrective measures in place. Birdye similarly complained that there was a dearth of programs and services for boys and girls between the ages of 14 and 21. She conceded that these youth could benefit from "some opportunity for recreation [and] for enjoyment" (Birdye Haynes, nd). Birdye Haynes knew that young African American boys were especially in need of services given their experiences with racial discrimination and lack of social and economic opportunities. Rather than turn "the gang" away, she emphasized the need to "divert these forces" and encouraged the boys to take an active and constructive role in Lincoln House. Her goal was to "so polish and refine . . . 'the gang' that others will say it is good for them to be here, and will come and cast in their lot with ours" (Haynes, 1915). Haynes sought a win-win situation with "the gang." In her opinion, the house would be functioning effectively if "the gang" could benefit from its programs, change their destructive behavior and become accepted community residents. The boys had to believe that they were welcomed and that workers at Lincoln House wanted them as participants. To that end, Birdye Haynes hired a Director of Boys' work and successfully recruited the boys into the House activities. In one of her reports to the board, Birdye Haynes later wrote that the new director had "stood all the tests of our examining board, 'the gang', and they have taken off their hats to him" (Haynes, 1915).

CONCLUSION

The type of community practice in which the Hayneses engaged can best be described as "race work." While their strategies, tactics, and approaches to community work mirror the organizer's profile that Rivera and Erlich (1992) ascribe to a skilled organizer and the generic processes of organizing, planning, development, and change which Weil (1994) describes as components of community practice, the Hayneses' perception of their labor was simply "race work" from a social science and social work perspective. A review of the Haynes' professionally directed "race work" reveals that it encompassed a range of community practice elements. According to Weil and Gamble's (1995) discussion of community practice, purposeful community organizing focuses on one or more of the following: (1) improving the quality of life, (2) advocacy, (3) human and economic development, (4) services and program planning, (5) service integration, (6) political and social action, and (7) social justice. The Haynes' community practice work focused on all of these elements.

First, their work had as its core *improving the quality* of life for all people but especially African Americans in urban areas. Birdye Haynes' work through the social settlements and George's through the NUL dealt with problems that individuals confronted in their quest to resettle in new and strange areas, such as finding employment and maintaining a healthy family life. Birdye's work also involved more complex activities such as organizing a kindergarten which allowed mothers to work and simultaneously protected children who would otherwise be left at home unsupervised.

Second, both of the Haynes embraced the role of *advocate–*

George on a national level and Birdye on a more regional or local level. Through the Fisk University Department of Social Sciences and the NUL, George Haynes advocated for the welfare of the community and established a social work program designed to train African American social workers to deal with the social problems that African Americans faced in urban areas. Through her settlement house work in both Chicago and New York, Birdye Haynes was a strong advocate for local community residents. Throughout her career, Birdye Haynes put the community's needs ahead of her own personal and professional goals. She constantly advocated for professionally trained workers and for services and programs to address the special needs of the new migrants who moved into the cities. She encouraged her board to seek to understand this unique group and to be sensitive to their background and culture.

Third, in an effort to encourage *human and economic develop-ment,* the social settlements with which Birdye was associated orga-nized mothers' clubs and men's clubs as well as other activities aimed at investing in human capital. The NUL engaged in training African American social workers.

Fourth, through *services and program planning,* the Haynes rec-ognized the African American community as an "emerging" popu-lation in urban centers. The array of services and programs which were made available to this population ranged from day care to opportunities for wholesome leisure to employment training to liter-ary circles for teaching and entertainment purposes. Teaching people to live successfully in cities was a task that both George and Birdye undertook in their respective work.

Fifth, the NUL grew out of a recognition of the importance of *service integration.* The organization resulted from the merger of three separate groups, the Committee for Improving Industrial Conditions for Negroes in New York, the National League for the Protection of Colored Women, and the Committee on Urban Condi-tions Among Negroes. This merger was motivated by the need for cooperation and harmonious collaboration in meeting the needs of an agrarian population moving into rapidly industrializing cities. For Birdye, the service integration work of the social settlement involved, for example, building a continuum of services for the welfare of women and girls through health care provision and "baby fairs" to teaching parenting skills and homemaking skills to Camp Fire Girls activities.

Sixth, part of the work of both the NUL and the social settlements involved *political and social action issues*. The NUL was very involved in helping employers to change their discriminatory hiring practices. Through meetings with specific employers, the organization's leaders would encourage various companies to hire African Americans. Later during the New Deal era, the federal government was targeted as the discriminating employer and similar strategies were used (Weiss, 1974). The executive director of the NUL at that time, Eugene K. Jones, became a member of President Roosevelt's informal "Black cabinet" working to ensure that the political process included people of color. Birdye, on a more individualized level, sometimes turned to her board for support to protect weaker members of the community. On one occasion, Birdye found that a young woman in the neighborhood, a teacher, who had become blind and had been obligated to give up her work, had applied for instruction in reading at the Light House of the New York Association for the Blind. The woman was denied assistance. Birdye believed that this denial of services was based on racism. She solicited advice from her board on the best way to intervene in behalf of the woman. The board responded by appointing a member to "take the matter up with the Light House" (Carlton-LaNey, 1994b). Birdye Haynes' advocacy for individuals was always done with an eye focused on greater social reform and social action.

Finally, the Haynes' careers reveal that work for *social justice* was a major aspect of community practice. They believed that it was the responsibility of all, regardless of race, to meet the needs of vulnerable groups. They also believed that the professionally trained African American social worker should have access to employment within any organization which served and met human needs. They theorized that organized interracial cooperation could lead to economic and social justice (Weiss, 1974). The Hayneses understood the value of their professional training and used it as an element fundamental to their "race work." For them, the race demanded and deserved their attention, and their professional knowledge and skills were only tools to help them to attack and ameliorate social problems that revolved around the exclusion and oppression of African Americans.

The Hayneses continued a lifetime of work in the African American community. George Haynes left Fisk University in 1918 to become Director of Negro Economics for the Department of Labor. In 1921 he became the Executive Secretary of the Commission on Race Relations for the Federal Council of Churches of America, a position that he held until his retirement in 1946. He died in 1960 at the age of 80. Birdye Haynes resigned from the Lincoln House Settlement in 1922 to accept a position with the Colored branch of the YWCA in New York City. She entered a hospital for surgery before she was to begin her new position, but died three weeks later at the age of 35 from heart failure (Carlton-LaNey, 1983, 1994b).

REFERENCES

Bulletin of the NLUCAN. (1915). p. 29.

Carlton-LaNey, I. (1994a). Introduction: the legacy of African-American leadership in social welfare. *Journal of Sociology and Social Welfare, 21*(1), 5-12.

Carlton-LaNey, I. (1994b). The career of Birdye Henrietta Haynes, a pioneer settlement house worker. *Social Service Review, 68*(2), 254-273.

Carlton-LaNey, I. (1994c). Training African-American social workers through the NUL fellowship program. *Journal of Sociology and Social Welfare, 21*(1), 43-53.

Carlton-LaNey, I. (1985). Fisk social work students' emergency relief work following the east Nashville fire of 1916. *Tennessee Historical Quarterly, 44*(4), 371-379.

Carlton-LaNey, I. (1984). George Edmund Haynes: A pioneer in social work. *Journal of Social and Behavioral Sciences, 30*(2), 39-47.

Carlton-LaNey, I. (1983). Notes on a forgotten Black social worker and sociologist: George Edmund Haynes. *Journal of Sociology and Social Welfare, 10*(3), 530-539.

Day, P. (1989). *A new history of social welfare.* New Jersey: Prentice Hall.

Drake, S., & Cayton, H.R. (1962). *Black metropolis.* New York: Harper and Row Publishers.

DuBois, W. E. B. (1903). The souls of Black folks. New York: Signet Classic Printing.

DuBois, W. E. B. (1912). Play for Negroes. *Survey,* 28, 614-642.

Fisk University Bulletin. (1913). p. 48. Nashville, TN.

Franklin, J. H., & Moss, A. A. (1994). *From slavery to freedom.* New York: McGraw Hill, Inc.

Fulks, B. (1969). *Black struggle.* New York: Dell Publishing Company.

Haynes, G. E. (undated) Memorandum of events connected with the fire relief development. In the James Weldon Johnson Collection, Box 5, Binecke Library, Yale University, New Haven Connecticut.

Haynes, G. E. (1911). Cooperation with colleges in securing and training Negro social workers for urban conditions. *Proceedings of the national conference of charities and corrections* 38 (June), 384-387.

Haynes, G. E. to Birdye Haynes. (1915, February 14). George Edmund Haynes Papers, Fisk University, Nashville, Tennessee.

Haynes, B. H. to George Haynes. (1915, April 17). George Edmund Haynes Papers, Fisk University, Nashville, Tennessee.

Haynes, B. H. to George Haynes, (1915, March 15). George Edmund Haynes Papers, Fisk University, Nashville, Tennessee.

Haynes, G. E. to Birdye Haynes, (1915, May 11). George Edmund Haynes Papers, Fisk University, Nashville, Tennessee.

Haynes, B. H. (1915). Report for December to the Lincoln House Board. Lillian Wald Papers, Butler Library, Columbia University, New York, New York.

Haynes, B. H. (1916-1917). Lincoln House Report 1916-17. Lillian Wald Papers, Butler Library, Columbia University, New York, New York.

Haynes, G. E. (1920, October 22). National Archives, Washington, D.C.

Haynes, B. H. (no date). Handwritten copy in the Julius Rosenwald Collection at the University of Chicago, Box 30.

Haynes, G. E. (1936). Private papers. Mt. Vernon, NY.

Jones, M. H. (1971). The responsibility of the Black college to the Black community: Then and now. *Daedalus, 100,* 732-744.

Kramer, R. M. (1967). Ideology, status, and power in board-executive relationships. In R. Kramer & H. Specht (Eds.), *Readings in community organization practice* (pp. 285-293). Englewood Cliffs, NJ: Prentice Hall, Inc.

Kogut, A. (1970). The Negro and the charity organization society in the progressive era. *Social Service Review, 44,* 11-21.

Lasch-Quinn, E. (1993). *Black neighbors race and the limits of reform in the American settlement house movement, 1890-1945.* North Carolina: The University of North Carolina Press.

Parris, G., & Brooks, L. (1971). *Blacks in the city.* Boston: Little, Brown and Company.

Popple, P. (1978). Community control of social work education: An historical example. *Journal of Sociology and Social Welfare, 5,* 152-167.

Rivera, F. G., & Erlich, J. L. (1992). Community organizing in a diverse society. Boston: Allyn and Bacon.

Ross, E. (1978). *Black heritage in social welfare 1860-1930.* New Jersey: The Scarecrow Press, Inc.

Siedner, V. M. (1969). Community organization in the direct-service agency. In Ralph Kramer & Harry Specht (Eds.), *Readings in community organization practice* (pp. 285-293). Englewood Cliffs, NJ: Prentice Hall, Inc.

Weil, M. & Gamble, D. (1995). Community practice models. In Richard Edwards

(Ed.), *Encyclopedia of Social Work,* Washington, DC: National Association of Social Workers Press.

Weil, M. (1994). Editor's introduction to the journal. *Journal of Community Practice, 1*(1), xxi-xxxiii.

Weiss, N. (1974). *The national urban league 1900-1940.* New York: Oxford University Press.

Lawrence Oxley
and Locality Development:
Black Self-Help in North Carolina
1925-1928

N. Yolanda Burwell, PhD

SUMMARY. In 1925, Lt. Lawrence Oxley became director of the Division of Work Among Negroes, a new unit of the North Carolina State Board of Charities and Public Welfare. The Division of Work Among Negroes was the first of its kind in the nation and it would become a model for other states to follow. Using locality development methods, Lt. Oxley stimulated significant public welfare initiatives among Blacks in thirty-eight counties before and during the early years of the Great Depression when North Carolina was a

N. Yolanda Burwell is Assistant Professor of Social Work at East Carolina University in Greenville, NC.

Address correspondence to: Dr. N. Yolanda Burwell, PhD, 216 A. Ragsdale, School of Social Work, East Carolina University, Greenville, NC 27858.

The author gratefully acknowledges the helpful suggestions of Drs. Iris Carlton-LaNey, Gary Lowe and Linner Griffith.

Partial funding for this research was provided by the Graduate School and Office of Vice Chancellor for Academic Affairs, East Carolina University.

A version of this article was presented at the 1991 annual meeting of the Association for the Study of African American Life and History.

The philanthropy among African Americans in various counties in North Carolina is more fully discussed in Burwell, N.Y. (1995). Shifting the Historical Lens: Early Economic Empowerment Among African Americans. *Journal of Baccalaureate Social Work, 1*(1), 25-37.

[Haworth co-indexing entry note]: "Lawrence Oxley and Locality Development: Black Self-Help in North Carolina 1925-1928." Burwell, N. Yolanda. Co-published simultaneously in *Journal of Community Practice* (The Haworth Press, Inc.) Vol. 2, No. 4, 1995, pp. 49-69; and: *African American Community Practice Models: Historical and Contemporary Responses* (ed: Iris Carlton-LaNey, and N. Yolanda Burwell) The Haworth Press, Inc., 1996, pp. 49-69. Single or multiple copies of this article are available from The Haworth Document Delivery Service [1-800-342-9678, 9:00 a.m. - 5:00 p.m. (EST)].

49

racially segregated state. Lawrence Oxley used the politics of Black self-help as a tool for fundamental social change in local public welfare activities. This article describes how his emphasis on Black self-help and indigenous leadership resulted in the placement and financing of the first Black social workers in public welfare offices in the state. *[Article copies available from The Haworth Document Delivery Service: 1-800-342-9678.]*

KEYWORDS. Self-help, locality development, African American community development, social welfare history

Community organization was not a well defined social work method when African American social worker Lieutenant Lawrence Oxley became director of the new Division of Work Among Negroes (the Division) in January, 1925. The Division was an experimental programmatic unit of the North Carolina State Board of Charities and Public Welfare and the first of its kind in the nation. It became a major vehicle for identifying leadership and community self-help initiatives among Black citizens in the state.

Lt. Oxley's community organization approach is the subject of this article. Using locality development methods, Lt. Oxley advanced community organization "with only the general principles of social work technic (sic) to guide the initial steps" of his work with the Division (North Carolina State Board of Charities and Public Welfare, 1926, p. 101). As director, Lawrence Oxley was responsible for documenting social conditions among Black North Carolinians and stimulating community problem solving among them to ameliorate distressing social conditions in the predominantly rural and racially segregated state. He successfully demonstrated that Black citizens across the state could organize themselves to work on local community betterment initiatives. His community organizing efforts resulted in the organization of welfare initiatives among Blacks in 38 counties, the employment of nearly one hundred Black welfare, health, farm and rural extension agents in the public sector, and the employment of 28 Black social workers (up from one) in county and city departments of public welfare before and during the Depression years (North Carolina State Board of Charities and Public Welfare, 1932, p. 101). Lt.

Oxley was so successful, other states sought his counsel on instituting public welfare for Black citizens.

This article describes Lt. Oxley's use of locality development strategies and his emphasis on self-help within the African American community. Three case examples of Oxley's community organization efforts in Alamance, Wake, and New Hanover counties are provided. Extant records from these counties provide important historical facts on the ways Blacks organized to secure the first Black social workers in their county welfare departments between 1925 and 1928. Newspaper accounts, city directories, biennial reports from the North Carolina State Board of Charities and Public Welfare also provide important details of Oxley's work. Finally, Oxley's professional writings in *The Southern Workman, North Carolina Teachers Record,* and administrative reports provide descriptions on fund raising, community character, indigenous leadership, and social structures during that time period.

CAREER OF LAWRENCE AUGUSTUS OXLEY

North Carolina's social welfare history often begins with the contributions by Howard Odum and the University of North Carolina on social work education, public welfare, and social science research.[1] The parallel contributions of pioneer social workers of color like Lawrence Oxley are too often obscured by time and systemic omission from the historical record. A correction of the omission is needed in order to fully understand North Carolina's social welfare history.

Lawrence Oxley contributed to the development of professional social work practice in North Carolina in three ways. He established a successful state social welfare agency concerned with the specific needs of Blacks; he organized citizens to remedy pressing social welfare needs at the local level; and he promoted social work education and training of Blacks through public welfare institutes and support of the Bishop Tuttle Memorial Training School of Social Work at St. Augustine's College in Raleigh. In this respect, Oxley advanced community organizing as a viable social work methodology when it was just emerging as a distinct social work intervention (Cox & Garvin, 1987, p. 47). As Gurin (1971) notes:

Community organization positions were manned for the most part by people who were not themselves professional social workers but had come into the field either with no professional training or from other backgrounds. Increasingly, however, as social work became professionalized, the people in community organization positions did identify themselves with the developing social work profession. (p. 1327)

This description characterizes Lawrence Oxley.

Born into a middle class family, Lawrence Oxley was privately educated in Boston. He did extensive military community service as one of the few Black Army morale officers during World War I (Pitts, 1934). He conducted social surveys on conditions among Blacks in major cities like Cincinnati, Washington, Chicago and Louisville. Prior to his appointment to the Division, he taught social science courses at St. Augustine College in Raleigh. These experiences qualified him as a "trained social worker" when he came to the Division.

Originally funded by the Laura Spelman Rockefeller Memorial Fund, the Division was set up to implement a state-wide public welfare program for Black citizens. It was a "venture in faith in the possibilities of a race to develop its own leaders and organize its social forces for community betterment . . ." (North Carolina State Board of Charities and Public Welfare, 1926, p. 101).

Lt. Oxley vigorously directed the Division for nine years. He was a can-do administrator and a strong believer in self-help among Blacks. Oxley (1927b, p. 17) insisted that "welfare work of a constructive nature" could not be "put over" on Blacks, but if it was to be worthwhile and permanent in character, Blacks had to fully understand and assume a large degree of responsibility for solving their own problems.

Tremendous strides were made in social welfare initiatives under his stewardship. Oxley advanced community organization as a social work method when professional practice methods were just evolving. He promoted the Division and community organization at social work conferences, public welfare institutes and through courses at the Bishop Tuttle Memorial Training School of Social Work, a professional school for Black females at St. Augustine's

College (Burwell, 1994; Gary & Gary, 1994). Articles on his methods and the Division appeared in major Black and Caucasian publications (Oxley,1925a; 1927b; 1931; 1929). Lt. Oxley's work was so significant that the state legislature made the Division of Work Among Negroes a permanent unit within the State Board of Charities and Public Welfare in 1931. William Johnson (1934-1943) and John Larkin (1943-1963) served as consultants with this unit until the early 1960s when segregated services were dismantled.

In 1934, Lt. Oxley joined the U.S. Department of Labor as Commissioner of Conciliation and Special Assistant to Secretary Frances Perkins. He was a member of President Roosevelt's Black Cabinet and a nationally recognized labor expert. Oxley retired from the federal government with over twenty years of service in 1957. He became national field coordinator for senior citizens during the Kennedy Administration. He directed special projects for the National Council of Senior Citizens (Man, 86, Oldest American to Head Fact-finding Unit, 1972). Lawrence Oxley died in 1973.

SELF-HELP

Today, Lt. Oxley's community organization model is called locality development. Practitioners of locality development mobilize a broad spectrum of people to set goals and execute realistic plans to achieve these goals. Through democratic problem-solving, local residents act in their own self-interests (Rothman & Tropman, 1987 p. 17). Themes of locality development include self-help, voluntary cooperation, development of indigenous leadership and educational agendas.

Stressing community organization rather than a psychoanalytic or casework approach, Lt. Oxley drew upon existing strengths and resources within counties, encouraged collective action among Blacks, and facilitated results. He believed in the ability of Blacks to decide and organize in their own self-interests. He also saw social workers as promoters of self-help.

> The purpose of a social worker in a Negro community is for the awakening of a social consciousness of the community to its needs and desire of self-help. The Negro social worker in

North Carolina, particularly in this (sic) pioneer days is expected to serve as probation officer, big sister and big brother to the underprivileged Negro child and be able to intelligently understand the social needs of the community and initiate programs of community service with which to satisfy, at least in part, these needs. (Lawrence Oxley to E. E. Smith, 1/11/28)

Self-help is not a new concept in social work; mutual aid, natural helping networks or social support systems are terms used to connote self-help among group members during times of need. Mutual aid is the expression of the need of people to have responsibility for each other's well-being (Johnson & Schwartz, 1988, p. 5). Before formal, professional services intervene, the responsibility of caring for others occurs through natural helpers (family, friends, neighbors, self), community benefits (churches and financial resources) and self-help groups (Johnson, 1995, p. 312-313).

Mutual aid seems to work most effectively when the people helping and being helped hold similar values, come from a similar culture, or have a similar life-style. The relationship between people can be one of sometimes helper, sometimes being helped. It is equalitarian and reciprocal. It has the advantage of being relatively nonintrusive, culturally relevant, fiscally inexpensive, nonstigmatizing, and relatively autmonous. (Johnson & Schwartz, 1988, p. 7)

Self-help held broader meanings for the Black community in the 1920s. Leaders like Marcus Garvey, Booker T. Washington, or Ida B. Wells-Barnett or scholars like Billingsley (1992) and Pollard (1978) do not characterize Black self-help as simply help. Self-help empowered many Blacks to achieve despite society's views of the race. Blacks were able to survive against harsh social conditions only through collective actions. Finally, self help was an act of defiance against oppression and exclusion. People refused to simply submit to the overt and covert dehumanization processes all around them.

The segregated society offered few services and opportunities for African American families. Consequently, survival depended on their ability to adapt to the various programs and policies of the several states that seemed determined to isolate, alienate, segregate, subordinate, or otherwise diminish their civic and social statute in the body politic. (Daly, Jennings, Beckett & Leashore, 1995, p. 243)

Blacks took matters into their own hands as much as possible to create decent lives for themselves and their less fortunate brothers and sisters. Therefore, rather than waiting for assistance from outsiders, Lt. Oxley believed Blacks were capable of taking care of their problems through cooperative work.

There are several examples of the kinds of problems that Lt. Oxley thought the community could address through cooperative work. For example, while inadequate services and an agrarian economy heightened serious social problems for many North Carolinians, Black citizens faced harsher circumstances and fewer service options due to oppressive segregation laws. Poverty, indecent housing, juvenile delinquency, crime and poor health conditions were much higher for Blacks than whites (Public Welfare in North Carolina, 1929; Oxley, 1929). Black children were especially vulnerable. Jail appeared to be their only service option. In 1925, 71 of the 138 children in jail under 16 years of age were Black. Of the 1,765 adolescents in jail between 16 and 21 years of age, 797 were Black (Children in Jail, 1925).

Emphasizing self-help was politically expedient for someone in Oxley's position in the 1920s for it answered many questions associated with providing county services to impoverished Blacks in a segregated, agrarian state. In 1917, North Carolina had restructured its public welfare system by making counties the central administrative unit. County welfare departments handled the growing problems of poverty, troubled children, and management of county welfare facilities. The State Board of Charities and Public Welfare had authority over one hundred county operations (Aydlette, 1947).

County public welfare services were rudimentary in 1925 when Lt. Oxley joined the Division. Staffing, organization, and record-keeping were lacking (North Carolina State Board of Charities and Public Welfare, 1926). State officials recognized the need to professionalize and increase public welfare operations, but funds and trained professionals were scarce, despite increasing demands for these services. In forty-six counties, the superintendent of public welfare did all the welfare work. In many counties, the superintendent serviced both the county welfare and school needs. Therefore, self-help among Blacks complemented evolving county services.

In addition, Black self-help did not disturb segregation laws or customs. "What must be avoided at all costs was an occasion that would even vaguely imply social equality" (Leyburn, 1989, p. 71).

> The fundamental assumption upon which all racial relations were based was that blacks (sic) are an inferior race. Although supposed evidence, anthropological and historical, underlay this conviction, to millions of Americans of the time [early 1920s] the inferiority of blacks was completely self-evident and axiomatic. Therefore, the mores forbade intermarriage, dating, or any other form of relationship that implied equality. Blacks and whites must have separate schools, churches, hospitals, clubs, eating places, railway cars and waiting rooms, toilet facilities. Where complete segregation was impossible . . . blacks must sit in the rear, or in theaters, in galleries or special sections. (Leyburn, 1989, p. 67-68)

Even the titles of Mister and Miss were not accorded to Blacks by Whites when addressing them, although the reverse was expected. Lt. Oxley retained his military title throughout his tenure in North Carolina so that he could be addressed with a proper title.

Caught in the southern fiction of serving White North Carolinians, without serving Blacks in the same or better manner, state and county officials faced an unsettling paradox. They acknowledged little had been done for Black citizens. Segregation laws exacerbated this situation (Aydlette, 1947; North Carolina State Board of Charities and Public Welfare, 1926; Sanders, 1933). However, many local and state officials understood that the failure to improve the well-being of one group could ultimately effect the well being of all (Welfare Workers for Negroes, 1928). Therefore, helping Blacks to take care of their own social ills at the county level was postured as race advancement rather than racial equality (Race Cooperation, 1926). The self-help model was constructed so that it did not overtly interfere with legal and customary segregation practices.

Black people fully understood the need for social welfare intervention in their communities. Martin and Martin (1985), Jones (1982), Pollard (1978) and Neverton-Morton (1989) document a long legacy of self-help and race uplift practices by Black churches, organizations and individuals to remedy problems. Oxley tapped into the intricacies and diversities of these social institutions and personalities with his community organization model. Being middle class, Oxley knew about the vital "machinery" of Black entrepreneurs, churches, lodges, men's and women's clubs that existed behind the veil of segregation in every hamlet and city. These men and women of the race often represented success and defied White notions of inferiority. They were educators, community builders and professionals engaged in uplift (self-help) work among the race.

> . . . those things by which the Negroes live–industry, education, health, social welfare–must be stimulated and developed. These interests are usually represented by organizations of some sort, such as the school, the church and the fraternal society. The only practical approach to these larger interests lies through the machinery of organizations Negroes themselves have set up. (Oxley, 1929, p. 8)

Lawrence Oxley (1929) also understood the flaws of the machinery. He lamented their marked separations, self-centered natures and apathy toward the general well-being of the total community. Though numerous, these groups as a rule worked independently and at times, were adversarial with each other. Social divisions within the race further exacerbated cooperative efforts. Businesses and services operated by representatives of the race struggled financially, had limited capacities, and were not statewide operations. Independently, they could not meet the many demands of Black citizens. For example, Black physicians founded many of the early Black hospitals in the state. The *University of North Carolina Newsletter* (Our Hospital Facilities, 1926) reports that out of 59 hospitals, nine existed for 763,400 Blacks in North Carolina, where a total of 353 beds were available. Black hospitals existed in Asheville, Durham, Gastonia, Charlotte, Wilmington, Henderson, Monroe and Raleigh.

Oxley's community organization approach drew on the existing self-help ethos among Blacks. His work validated and strengthened Black community problem-solving and capabilities. Unity, cooperation, and constructive action among groups were the aim. Community organizing was a way to "unite existing groups for work rather than bring(ing) something new, which would be an additional burden to what is, in most cases an already overloaded community" (Oxley, 1929, pp. 8-9).

Lt. Oxley's use of locality development provided a means of advancing a group without upsetting southern social codes between the races. His approach encouraged collective work and prosocial behavior among Black organizations and individuals to organize parent-teacher associations, recreational services and to support institutions serving the race. All such efforts augmented the limited public welfare services available to Blacks. The success of Lt. Oxley's model was considered extraordinary even during his time and very positive for the state.

OXLEY'S COMMUNITY ORGANIZATION PLAN

In 1925 community organization was not a clearly defined social work methodology and locality development was an untested model. Locality development themes of indigenous leadership, educational agendas, and voluntary cooperation were evident in Lt. Oxley's community organization approach. Broad county participation among Blacks and key Whites was necessary. The model involved a cross-section of county representatives, including newspaper editors, school children, ministers and businessmen. Lt. Oxley charted this new approach and validated its effectiveness through practice, published reports and educational forums.

Lt. Oxley went into communities to organize only when he was invited. Initially, county officials like Wake County Welfare Superintendent Fannie Bickett sought Oxley's services as part of the North Carolina Plan.[2] As his success grew, other counties and groups sought his counsel to organize local citizens.

Lt. Oxley helped local leaders to identify priorities and community needs first. He believed strongly that the intelligent study of Black problems should guide planning and intervention. Local needs were studied. In some cases, he surveyed the community; at other times, the work had already been done.

In Oxley's locality development model, central leadership rested with the county Negro Advisory Committee, a small group of influential Black citizens who were creditable to both Blacks and Whites. These citizens were selected by county officials; sometimes Oxley had input on this selection process. These astute local bodies were an important part of the community organization model because they implemented the plan of action among Blacks and negotiated with county officials. Within each county, these indigenous county leaders assumed full responsibility for meeting their self-defined goals. Lt. Oxley assumed an advisor role once the county's Negro Advisory Committee was fully operating.

Education and public relations were characteristic features of his approach. Newspaper coverage, public notices, and mass meetings kept the program of organization in the public's eye. His approach respected Black and Caucasian leadership and idiosyncrasies within each county.

The basic steps of Oxley's community organization plan (1929) are outlined in Figure 1. Repeated implementation of his approach produced predictable results. The model was practical. Full execution took about three months. By the time Oxley left North Carolina in 1934, thirty-eight counties had been organized or were in the process of being organized with this approach.

Extant records from Oxley's work in Wake, Alamance, and New Hanover counties illuminate the various aspects of the community organizing plan from 1925 to 1928. The Wake County case study describes Lt. Oxley's debut and the division of labor the Negro Advisory Committee used to canvass the townships. The Alamance County case illustration details how Black individuals, churches, and organizations were financially assessed in the townships to raise private funds to provide public welfare support for the Black communities. By the time Lt. Oxley went to New Hanover County in 1928, one sees a well-tested model in operation. Here the specific involvements of Lt. Oxley with various community leaders is highlighted and the level of community response is recorded.

FIGURE 1. Lawrence Oxley's Model for Locality Development

1. Welfare superintendents or other officials invited Lt. Oxley to the county to organize Blacks.

2. He held several meetings with welfare officials and Black leaders to engage their interest in a proposed welfare program.

3. A study of local needs and resources was made by Black citizens where strengths and capabilities of Black organizations were identified.

4. County representatives and race leaders then adopted a proposed welfare program, usually to secure a Black social worker.

5. A Negro Advisory Committee was appointed by the county welfare superintendent and functioned as an auxiliary group to the County Board of Public Welfare and the county welfare superintendent.

6. The Negro Advisory Committee met regularly with the county officials. Strategies for raising private and public funds to finance a full time trained Black social worker and other necessary items in the promotion of county wide welfare programs was discussed. Lt. Oxley moved to an advisor role, once the county's Negro Advisory Committee began operating.

7. Once the funds were secured, a trained Black social worker was hired upon the approval of the State Welfare Commissioner, Mrs. Kate Burr Johnson.

8. Following this appointment, interracial and intraracial group meetings were held in community centers to educate the public about new welfare worker (Larkin, nd).

WAKE COUNTY

Wake County was the first to establish a public welfare program for Blacks using Oxley's community organization approach. It had been one of the four counties selected for the North Carolina Plan to build up its county welfare services. Wake County had 75,155 residents and held the capital city of Raleigh. Blacks comprised 41% of the population (North Carolina State Board of Charities and Public Welfare, 1926, p. 109).

Wake County's newly appointed Superintendent of Public Welfare, Mrs. Fannie Yarborough Bickett, invited Lt. Oxley to meet with representatives of the race to discuss welfare problems. Oxley met with Mrs. Bickett and members of the local Negro Advisory Committee on January 8, 1925. Dr. Lemuel T. Delany, Mrs. Addie L. Alexander, Britton Pearce, Miss Margie Pascal, and Berry O'Kelly formed the committee. Dr. Delany was a noted Raleigh surgeon. Mrs. Alexander was a wealthy clubwoman and well known for her welfare and civic activities (Negro Leader Dies at her Home Here, 1931). Berry O'Kelly was the leading Black merchant in the county and founder of an accredited high school (*Paths Toward Freedom*, 1976, p. 177). Britton Pearce owned and operated a successful grocery. Margie Pascal was a respected teacher in a rural school.

After studying Wake county, the Negro Advisory Committee, county officials, and Oxley identified five welfare agendas. These included (a) the ways and means to finance the salary and expenses of a Negro worker; (b) study of the violations to and enforcement of the Compulsory School Attendance Law; (c) endowment of a bed at St. Agnes Hospital, the Black hospital; (d) publicity about the state welfare programs at meetings, clubs, conventions, newspapers, and parent-teacher associations and (e) correlation of the county welfare program with state and city programs (Oxley, 1925b).

Smaller meetings were held in outlying sections of the county after this initial meeting. The Negro Advisory Committee continued to meet and study the social needs of Wake County Blacks. The committee presented a suggested program with a budget of $1500. The program was informally adopted by state and county officials.

The county was divided into 18 townships. Within each township Mrs. Bickett appointed three persons to act as liaisons to the Negro Advisory Committee. No doubt identified by Oxley and the Negro Advisory Committee, liaisons included ministers, teachers, club-women, and other esteemed members of the race. Success for meeting the goal was dependent upon Blacks fully understanding and supporting the welfare objective before them. Each liaison had the task of keeping the objectives of the program before their township and collecting a designated amount of funds to meet their proposed goal. Mass meetings were held in each township and the county wide program was explained in detail.

This plan of organization netted $900 in cash and $500 in pledges from townships. These funds were given to county officials with the understanding that a Black social worker would be hired when the remaining $100 was raised (Oxley, 1925b; Larkin, nd, p. 6).

On September 1, 1925, Margery Edwards joined Mrs. Bickett's office as a probation officer and caseworker for Black youth. With seven years of experience with the Episcopal City Mission in Phila-delphia, Ms. Edwards became Wake County's first Black welfare worker. Mrs. Bickett credited Lt. Oxley with securing Edward's position and funds for her salary (Negroes To Have Welfare Worker, 1925, p. 5). Black citizens supplied Miss Edward's $1500 annual salary and transportation costs for the first year. The city of Raleigh and Wake County paid her salary the following years.

ALAMANCE COUNTY

Alamance County organized for welfare among Blacks in the fall of 1925. The textile company, Burlington Industries, was the county's major employer. Over 32,700 people resided in the Pied-mont county; a fourth of them were Black (North Carolina State Board of Charities and Public Welfare, 1926, p. 109).

Five people served on the Alamance County Negro Advisory Committee. Alamance County was divided into thirteen townships. Each township was assigned three liaisons to keep the program before the people and collect the funds.

Lt. Oxley's administrative notes (1925c) detail the number and type of organizations and people canvassed in rural counties like Alamance. Black churches, organizations and key individuals were financially assessed to meet the goal of $1000. Thirty-eight churches were assessed $15 or $25. Thirty lodges and fraternal groups like the Odd Fellows, Knight of Pythias, and Eastern Star were assessed $25. Eleven individuals were expected to give $10. Fifty teachers were to give $1 each and 1500 school children were to give five cents. The total assessments came to over $1500. A county wide mass meeting was scheduled for November 8, 1925 at 4:00 pm at the Alamance Court House to inform people of this welfare program.

The chair of the Negro Advisory committee, Rev. Simon G. Walker became a part-time worker with the county welfare department. His salary was paid by Blacks (North Carolina State Board of Charities and Public Welfare, 1926).

NEW HANOVER COUNTY

By 1927, under Oxley's leadership nineteen counties had organized or were in the process of organizing for all kinds of welfare work among Blacks. Fourteen Blacks were employed in full time positions in nine counties as probation officers, family caseworkers, welfare assistants, and community organizers. This successful record prompted Blacks in New Hanover County to organize their welfare program. The port city of Wilmington was the only city of its size without a welfare program for Blacks (Welfare Work for Negroes, 1928). Nearly 41,000 people lived in the coastal North Carolina county; Blacks made up 48% of the population (North Carolina State Board of Charities and Public Welfare, 1926, p. 109).

William. P. McGlaughan, Superintendent of Public Welfare, and Dr. Frank W. Avant of the Colored Chamber of Commerce invited Lt. Oxley to Wilmington. Lt. Oxley met with a hand picked group of 18 Black citizens to outline procedures of the community organization model on November 29, 1927. The group decided to raise $1000 of $1800 to hire a Black welfare worker. The balance of $800 would come from city and state funds. Oxley's administrative notes (1928) detail the proposed budget:

Salary of worker	$90 per month	$1080
Ford runabout		350
Upkeep of the Ford car		200
Relief or Emergency Fund		170
Total budget for one year beginning July 1, 1928		$1800

On January 15, 1928, three hundred people heard the purpose of welfare work among Blacks at St. Stephens Methodist Church from Lt. Oxley and others. Reasons for raising $1000 were outlined. Representatives or captains from churches and fraternal organizations were appointed.

Over the next week, Oxley met with captains at Gregory Public

School to receive their first reports of the canvass. He conferred with editors of the city's two white papers, the *Wilmington Star* and the *News Dispatch,* to promote the plan; hearty cooperation was assured. He visited Mr. Louis T. Moore, executive secretary of the Wilmington Chamber of Commerce, and received his endorsement. Lt. Oxley held separate meetings with County Commissioners, the Mayor, and City Finance Commissioner. He conferred with Board of Education members and YMCA representatives about this endeavor. He also spoke with Supt. McGlaughan and Mrs. W. L. Parsley, a County Welfare Board member.

At a community meeting on January 20, 1928, Rev. William H. Moore, Mrs. Sadie B. Davis, Mrs. Josie Taylor, Mrs. Robert S. Jervay, John T. Belden, Professor David C. Virgo, and Dr. Frank Avant were elected to the permanent Negro Advisory Committee. Dr. Avant was a prominent physician in Wilmington. Mr. Virgo was principal of Williston Industrial School. Mr. Belden was a printer. Mrs. Jervay's family published the *Cape Fear Journal,* the city's Black newspaper. Mrs. Davis's family ran the funeral home and Rev. Moore was pastor of Shiloh Baptist Church.

This campaign was significant enough for the *Wilmington Morning Star* to note "The session marked the first time that the negro (sic) factions in the eastern and western factions of the city have been brought together" (Final Report to be Made on Drive for Social Event, 1928). On Sunday, sixteen hundred people attended a mass meeting at St. Lukes Methodist Church. The goal of $1000 was realized (Oxley, 1928).

State Commissioner Kate Burr Johnson approved the appointment of Miss Carrie G. Hargrave as a full time welfare worker in the New Hanover County Welfare Office in September, 1928. She was in "charge of the school children in the negro (sic) institutions and all other work pertaining to the welfare of the negro (sic) element in Wilmington" (Carrie Hargrave Begins Her Work as Social Agent, 1928, p. 5).

CONCLUSION

Five factors enabled Lt. Lawrence Oxley to successfully organize Blacks to act in their own self-interest around pressing social needs throughout the state of North Carolina. First, urgent and growing social service needs existed among Blacks. Limited resources and Jim Crow laws prohibited full and equitable participation of existing services to ameliorate those problems fully.

Secondly, the inequity of services was not lost on some Caucasian officials. Certain individuals clearly chose to do something about it. For example, the progressive stances of Mrs. Bickett in Wake County and Commissioner Johnson at the state level allowed this work to exist and supported the execution of the plan to develop public welfare services for Black communities. Certain counties did not extend to Lt. Oxley the opportunity to do this work.

Thirdly, the approach tapped into the resource systems and helping tradition among Blacks. Organizations and institutions cooperated to meet mutual goals which benefitted all. Everyone contributed what they could and experienced victories because of their efforts. Black citizens paid salaries, transportation costs, and other expenses for early welfare workers to maximize their success in local communities. Blacks engaged in proactive and positive social behaviors with this approach.

Fourth, Black citizens were informed of and participated in county affairs. The social welfare aims and agendas were kept before people through mass meetings, committee work, and liaisons working in townships. Oxley understood the work could not be "put over on people" or dictated to them. Therefore, his approach kept the objectives and needs in front of the people all the time and they responded.

Finally, the Negro Advisory Committees allowed Black leaders to deliberate on county and state operations as they impacted on Black citizens. These committees wielded enormous influence and had growing impact over the years as the state wrestled with economic depression and high unemployment.

> Every effort has been made to mobilize all Negro church, fraternal and business organizations into a combined and articulate working arrangement to meet the economic strain on thousands of underprivileged people. It was felt at the onset that unless competent Negroes were appointed and authorized to function as participating members of local relief commit-

tees, the true facts regarding Negro unemployment and their relationship to the larger problems of community and state unemployment could not be intelligently studied and a constructive and practical program of relief promoted. (North Carolina State Board of Charities and Public Welfare, 1932, p. 100-101)

For nine years Lt. Oxley demonstrated how organized community participation stimulated self-help in southern Black communities and increased a Black welfare workforce. In mobilizing the positive forces within the Black community, Oxley (1927a) sought to stimulate improvements in schools, community centers and housing. For example, he worked with Jeanes supervisors, predecessors of cooperative extension workers, in rural schools to increase the Black parent-teacher associations. These associations supplied needs that ranged from transportation services to building and beautification projects. Commenting on Black self-help, Oxley (1931, p. 349) said ". . . they have given generously of their slender means to help pay for trained workers, for building at our training schools, for reclaiming delinquent youth and for the support of community chests."

Citizen participation in county and township affairs hold just as much relevance today as then. The alarm over AIDS, school drop-out rates, hypertension, violence and drug abuse in Black communities are the pressing and complicated issues of today. The underutilization of services and the barriers people experience trying to use services today parallel the inequities of the 1920s and 1930s.

The entrepreneurial and philanthropic spirit is active in the Black community. Individuals, businesses and professional groups, fraternal organizations, churches and college alumni from historically Black institutions are just some of the sources of aid. Blacks operate after school programs, tutorial services, informal home health care for Black elders and children in the community; these are examples of mutual aid. However, traditional social work agencies seldom turn to these bodies for aid or collaboration. This oversight clouds thinking and hinders effective community problem-solving with Blacks.

Lt. Oxley practiced from a strengths perspective and capitalized on the collective forces within the community. His strong belief in self-help was a protest and survival strategy. Blacks were not victims. They could and should create services for themselves. Doing for self was an act of solidarity and community power. Social work facilitated this change process and African Americans experienced significant victories for the race. Too much of social work practice today focuses on individual responsibility rather than community change processes. Oxley's methods remind us of the value and power of community action. Community practice remains a viable and needed social work method with people who have institutions, leaders, and aspirations.

NOTES

1. Noted sociologist Howard Odum founded the School of Social Work at the University of North Carolina-Chapel Hill and made a significant influence on the development of social work throughout the state. He was a catalyst in advancing a county system of public welfare services in North Carolina, fostering interracial cooperation and promoting trained social workers in the field. See Blackwell, J. & Janowitz, M. (1974) *Black Sociologists–Historical and Contemporary Perspective.* Chicago: University of Chicago Press, pp. 144-146

2. Funded by the Laura Spelman Rockefeller Memorial Fund for $30,000 for a three year period, the North Carolina Plan was a cooperative venture with the University of North Carolina's school of public welfare and the State Board of Charities and Public Welfare to strengthen the organization of public welfare services and train students of social work. Wake, Chatham, Buncombe and Orange counties were selected to test out the proposal.

REFERENCES

Aydlette, A. (1947). The North Carolina State Board of Public Welfare. *The North Carolina Historical Review, 24,* 33.
Billingsley, A. (1992). *Climbing Jacob's ladder.* New York: Simon & Schuster.
Burwell, N. (1994). North Carolina Public Welfare Institutes for Negroes 1926-1946. *Journal of Sociology and Social Welfare, 21,* 55-66.
Carrie Hargrave begins her work as social agent. (1928, September) *The Wilmington Morning Star,* p. 5
Children in jail (1925, April 8) *University of North Carolina Newsletter,* p. 1
Cox, F. & Garvin, C. (1987). A history of community organizing since the civil war with special reference to oppressed communities. In F. Cox, J. Erlich, J. Rothman & J. Tropman (Eds.) *Strategies of community organization* (pp.45-75). Itasca, IL: F. E. Peacock.

Daly, A., Jennings, J., Beckett, & Leashore, B. (1995). Effective coping strategies of African Americans. *Social Work, 40,* 240-248.

Final report to be made on drive for social event (1928, January) *Wilmington Morning Star,* society, p. 1.

Gary, R. & Gary L. (1994). The history of social work education for black people 1900-1930. *Journal of Sociology and Social Welfare, 21,* 67-81.

Gurin, A. (1971). Social planning and community organization. *Encyclopedia of Social Work.* Washington, D.C.: National Association of Social Workers, 1324-1337.

Johnson, L. (1995). *Social work practice–A generalist approach.* Boston: Allyn and Bacon.

Johnson, L. & Schwartz, C. (1988). *Social welfare–A response to human need.* Boston: Allyn and Bacon.

Jones, B. (1982). Mary Church Terrell and the National Association of Colored Women, 1896 to 1901. *Journal of Negro History, 67,* 20-33.

Larkin, J. (nd) *A history of the unit of work among negroes.* Raleigh: North Carolina Board of Charities and PublicWelfare.

Leyburn, J. (1989). *The way we lived-Durham 1900-1920.* Elliston, Va: North-cross House Publishers.

Man, 86, oldest American to head fact-finding unit (1972, September 21) *Jet,* p. 10.

Martin, E. & Martin, J. (1985). *The helping tradition in the black family and the community.* Silver Springs, MD: NASW.

Negro leader dies at her home here. (1931, December). *The News and Observer.* p. 2

Negroes to have welfare worker. (1925, September). *The News and Observer* p. 5

Neverton-Morton, C. (1989). *Afro-American women of the south and the advancement of the race 1895-1925* Knoxville: The University of Tennessee Press.

North Carolina State Board of Charities and Public Welfare. (1924). *Biennial Report of the North Carolina State Board of Charities and Public Welfare July 1, 1922 to June 30, 1924.* Raleigh: North Carolina State Board of Charities and Public Welfare.

North Carolina State Board of Charities and Public Welfare. (1926). *Biennial Report of the North Carolina State Board of Charities and Public Welfare July 1, 1924 to June 30, 1926.* Raleigh: North Carolina State Board of Charities and Public Welfare.

North Carolina State Board of Charities and Public Welfare. (1928). *Biennial Report of the North Carolina State Board of Charities and Public Welfare July 1, 1926 to June 30, 1928.* Raleigh: North Carolina State Board of Charities and Public Welfare.

North Carolina State Board of Charities and Public Welfare. (1930). *Biennial Report of the North Carolina State Board of Charities and Public Welfare July 1 1928 to June 30, 1930.* Raleigh: North Carolina State Board of Charities and Public Welfare.

North Carolina State Board of Charities and Public Welfare. (1932). *Biennial Report of the North Carolina State Board of Charities and Public Welfare July*

1, 1930 to June 30, 1932. Raleigh: North Carolina State Board of Charities and Public Welfare.

North Carolina State Board of Charities and Public Welfare. (1934). *Biennial Report of the North Carolina State Board of Charities and Public Welfare July 1, 1932 to June 30, 1934.* Raleigh: North Carolina Board of Charities and Public Welfare.

Our Hospital Facilities. (1926, June 12). *The University of North Carolina Newsletter.*

Oxley, L. to Smith, E., 1/11/28. Unit of Work Among Negroes Papers. North Carolina Division of Archives and History.

Oxley, L. (1925a). Negro welfare and progress in North Carolina. *The Southern Workman, 54,* 516-20

Oxley, L. (1925b) *Special report–Bureau of work among negroes January 1 to March 31, 1925.* Box 234. Unit of Work Among Negroes Papers. North Carolina Division of Archives and History.

Oxley, L. (1925c) *Suggested outline of organization of welfare work among negroes in Alamance County, North Carolina.* Box 4. Bureau of Work Among Negroes Papers, Alamance County folder. North Carolina Division of Archives and History.

Oxley, L. (1927a). The North Carolina negro. *Welfare Magazine.* Reprinted by the North Carolina State Board of Charities and Public Welfare.

Oxley, L. (1927b). North Carolina's welfare program for negroes. *The Southern Workman, 56,* 16-25.

Oxley, L. (1928). *Notes on the organization of public welfare work among negroes in New Hanover County.* Box 4. Bureau of Work Among Negroes Papers. New Hanover County folder. North Carolina Division of Archives and History.

Oxley, L. (1929). Organizing the North Carolina negro community. *The Southern Workman, 58,* 3-11.

Oxley, L. (1931). North Carolina's venture in negro welfare. *The Southern Workman, 60,* 348-351.

Oxley, L.(1932) Unemployment relief in North Carolina. *North Carolina Teachers Record, 32,* 36-37.

Paths toward freedom–A biographical history of Blacks and Indians in North Carolina by Blacks and Indians (1976). Raleigh: Center for Urban Affairs NCSU.

Pitts, L. (1934, May) New Deal personalities. *Journal and Guide* p. 6.

Pollard, W. (1978). *A study of Black self-help* San Francisco: R & E Associates.

Race Cooperation (1926, January 13). *The University of North Carolina Newsletter.*

Rothman, J. & Tropman J. (1987). Models of community organization and macro practice perspectives: Their mixing and phasing. In F. Cox, J. Erlich, J. Rothman & J. Tropman (Eds.) *Strategies of community organization* (pp. 3-26). Itasca, IL: F. E. Peacock.

Sanders, W. (1933). *Negro child welfare in North Carolina.* Chapel Hill: University of North Carolina Press for North Carolina State Board of Charities and Public Welfare.

Welfare workers for negroes. (1928, January) *Wilmington Morning Star,* p. 4.

HIV/AIDS Prevention
in the African American Community:
An Integrated Community-Based
Practice Approach

Irene Luckey, DSW

SUMMARY. The high rate of AIDS cases among African Americans, especially women, suggests that HIV risk reduction behavior change programs and messages have not been highly successful in preventing HIV transmission among this population. This paper recommends that the situational and environmental context of African Americans' lives, and their responses to HIV/AIDS be addressed and incorporated into HIV prevention programs in an effort to make these programs more relevant to high risk African Americans. A multi-level system intervention approach grounded in an ecosystem perspective which focuses on the community as the primary target level of intervention is proposed to increase the effectiveness of HIV prevention efforts among African Americans. *[Article copies available from The Haworth Document Delivery Service: 1-800-342-9678.]*

KEYWORDS. African Americans, HIV/AIDS, prevention, community, community-based practice, integrated practice, forum

Irene Luckey is Assistant Professor of Social Work at Rutgers University.

Address correspondence to: Irene Luckey, DSW, School of Social Work, Rutgers University, 536 George St., New Brunswick, NJ 08903.

Support for this research was provided by Rutgers University Minority Faculty Development Grant.

[Haworth co-indexing entry note]: "HIV/AIDS Prevention in the African American Community: An Integrated Community-Based Practice Approach." Luckey, Irene. Co-published simultaneously in *Journal of Community Practice* (The Haworth Press, Inc.) Vol. 2, No. 4, 1995, pp. 71-90; and: *African American Community Practice Models: Historical and Contemporary Responses* (ed: Iris Carlton-LaNey, and N. Yolanda Burwell) The Haworth Press, Inc., 1996, pp. 71-90. Single or multiple copies of this article are available from The Haworth Document Delivery Service [1-800-342-9678, 9:00 a.m. - 5:00 p.m. (EST)].

The epidemic of acquired immune deficiency syndrome (AIDS) has been recognized in the United States since 1981 (Jonsen & Stryker, 1993). Since that time, 401,749 cases of AIDS have been reported to the Center for Disease Control and Prevention (CDC) (CDC, 1994). As of June 1994, the number of AIDS cases among African Americans totaled 127,183; 99,502 were males and 27,681 were females (CDC, 1994).

The prevalence of AIDS cases varies among different segments of the at-risk populations. The growth in the number of AIDS cases in the gay community has decreased while African Americans and Latinos remain disproportionately affected by the epidemic. Through mid-1993, 48% of all AIDS cases reported were African Americans and Latinos, although these two groups comprise only 21% of the U.S. population (CDC, 1993a).

The fastest growth rate of AIDS is among African American and Latina women. Seventy-four percent of all women with AIDS are Black and Latina (CDC, 1993b). In New Jersey alone, among the new cases of AIDS in women, 64% are African Americans and it is the leading cause of death for African Americans between the ages of 15-44 years (New Jersey Women and AIDS Network, 1994). HIV infection among women also affects the number of pediatric AIDS cases. Seventy-nine percent of the AIDS cases among children 13 years or less are Black and Latino (CDC, 1993b).

Nationally and locally much has been done since 1981 to inform and educate the public about the modes of HIV transmission, at risk behaviors, and HIV prevention strategies and techniques. Individual level risk reduction behavior change is the primary focus of most existing messages and methods to inform and educate the general population about HIV/AIDS transmission and prevention. Although risk reduction behavior change messages have contributed to the success of stabilizing and/or decreasing the rate of HIV transmission with some segments of the population, the data suggest that the individual level risk reduction behavior change approach as the only method of intervention is not highly effective with all segments of the population. Becker and Joseph (1988) note that influencing behavior change is dependent on psychological, sociological, and cultural determinants. This paper proposes an integrated methods practice approach for dealing with HIV/AIDS treatment and education in the African American community. This method focuses on the community as the target of intervention and is grounded in an ecosystem perspective informed by cultural knowledge and responsiveness. Engaging a number of systems simultaneously in an education and change process that reflects cultural sensitivity is a more appropriate strategy to help decrease the transmission of HIV among African Americans.

AFRICAN AMERICANS' RESPONSE TO HIV/AIDS

Perceptions of HIV/AIDS as a White Gay Male Disease

When HIV/AIDS was first publicized, it was viewed primarily as a gay male disease by the medical authorities and the public at large. Early on the gay community was actively involved in publicizing HIV/AIDS and disseminating information about factors associated with the transmission of the disease. Much of the information was specifically targeted to gays and the gay community. Mainly as a result of the widespread beliefs and attitudes of African Americans that "HIV/AIDS is not my problem; it's a white gay male problem," high-risk African Americans did not readily embrace or adopt behavioral changes that reduce the risk of HIV infection from 1981 until 1986 (Jenkins, Lamar, & Thompson-Crumble, 1993). Denial by African Americans that gays, lesbians, and bisexuals exist in the African American community further reduced open responsiveness and outreach efforts to prevent the spread of HIV/AIDS (Quimby, 1993).

Mistrust of Medical Establishment

The long existing mistrust and skepticism that the African American community has had with the medical and other institutional establishments have affected receptivity of African Americans to HIV risk reduction behavior change messages. Suspicion, curiosity, rumors, and concern continue to exist in the African American community about the origin of the virus (Is the virus a result of a conspiracy to reduce and/or eliminate the Black population? [genocide]); where it originated (Did the virus originate in Africa?); and is there a cure (Does a cure exist that is being withheld until the goals of a genocidal conspiracy have been fulfilled?) (Thomas & Quinn, 1991; Dalton, 1989). Jenkins et al. (1993) indicate that the history of public health programs in the African American community has been less than positive, thus contributing to the lack of responsiveness to messages to prevent the transmission of HIV. Experiences and stories of African Americans being involuntarily sterilized and being used as subjects in studies to reduce fertility are well known in the community. The notoriety of the Tuskegee experimental study which documented the progression of syphilis in a southern Black male population without offering any treatment is perhaps the most salient U.S. example of the abuse of a minority population in a "scientific experiment." Knowledge of this experiment is widespread in the African American community and contributes to continuing mistrust of health interventions and studies.

Competing Risk Factors

In addition, the African American community has not responded well to HIV risk reduction behavior change messages and models because many competing survival issues and needs exist in the community which may be viewed as putting one at greater risk than HIV/AIDS infection. Poverty, high rates of unemployment, drugs, health risks such as heart disease, strokes, cancer, diabetes, poor access to health care, violence, and crime are only some of the high risk factors confronting African Americans daily (U.S. Department of Health and Human Services, 1985). The National Center for Health Statistics (1994) reports that the death rate from heart disease is higher among Blacks than any other ethnic group. Black males have the highest death rate from unintentional injuries; lung cancer mortality rate is highest among Black males, and the death rate from strokes is highest among Blacks. Villarosa (1994) highlights major health problems Black women encounter.

> Black women live fewer years than white women. Our breast cancer is caught later, and we are more likely to die from it. The majority of women and children infected with HIV disease are Black. Our children are more likely to be born small, and they die more frequently before reaching one year of age.

We have heart disease at younger ages, a heart attack is more likely to prove fatal, and we have twice as many cases of high blood pressure as whites. Nearly 50% of us are overweight. We are more likely to smoke, and we are less likely to quit than white women. We have higher rates of sexually transmitted infection and pelvic inflammatory disease. Over half of us have been beaten, been raped, or survived incest. (p. xvi)

Some health reports have argued that the stresses of poverty, economic oppression, lack of opportunity, and racism contribute significantly to health problems in the African American community (Beardsley, 1990; Jaynes & Williams, 1989; U.S Department of Health and Human Services, 1985). Others have argued that mistrust of the medical system, combined with a level of fatalism about major health problems, contributes to these health issues (Cummings, 1969; Jackson, 1981; Jenkins, Lamar, & Thompson-Crumble, 1993). When many African American families and communities face the daily oppression of poverty, unemployment, and pressing survival issues as well as the realities of prevalent, better known, and better understood major health problems, it is more understandable that HIV/AIDS has not been viewed with the same urgency as it has in some other communities.

African American Community Experiences Related to HIV/AIDS

The most prevalent mode of transmission of HIV is intravenous drug use (IVDU) for both males and females. According to the HIV/AIDS Surveillance Report (CDC, 1994), 37% of the 99,502 Black males with AIDS and 51% of the 27,681 females with AIDS acquired it through IVDU. Controversy and opposition from some African American leaders continue to exist about needle exchange programs. Where widespread speculation exists about conspiracies against African Americans, needle-exchange programs are viewed as cheap and cynical substitutes for drug-treatment programs that governments persistently refuse to pay for (Kirp & Bayer, 1993).

The second most prevalent mode of transmission of HIV for Black females is heterosexual contact; 33% of Black females acquire HIV through heterosexual contact while this is true for only 5% of Black males. For Black males, 41% become infected through sexual contact with other men (CDC, 1993a). Richie (1990) asserts that the prevailing societal view of Black women's sexuality as promiscuous, irresponsible, and involved in illicit sexual activity such as prostitution has made the community defensive and hesitant to openly discuss any issue related to sexuality. She suggests that this silence has left Black women particularly vulnerable to HIV infection because of a lack of opportunities to discuss sexual behavior and AIDS risks.

Socio-political and economic environments also affect interpersonal relationships and survival strategies used by African Americans. Thus the nature and purpose of sexual relationships may be quite complex, contributing to the increased rate of HIV/AIDS among African American women despite HIV risk reduction behavior change messages. Women may engage in unprotected sex with their partner because they lack adequate skills or do not feel empowered to negotiate effectively with their partner about the use of condoms. They may need financial support from their partner or several partners in order to provide for their children and themselves. African American males are likely to view birth control as the responsibility of the women. The insistence on the use of a condom may be viewed by the male as a lack of trust in his fidelity to the relationship. When the insistence on condom use is viewed as putting the relationship at risk, some women opt to have unprotected sex in order to keep the relationship although they are aware of potential health risks.

Denial of homosexuality and bisexuality in the African American community also hinders HIV/AIDS prevention efforts. Concerns about internal and external views of the African American community regarding homosexuality and bisexuality complicate efforts to directly deal with HIV/AIDS prevention and treatment. There are interrelated social, psychological, and political issues and perspectives operating in this complex area that range beyond the focus of this paper. A groundbreaking analysis of these important and complex issues has been provided by H.L. Dalton in a 1989 article in *Daedalus* on AIDS and gays in the African American community.

AN INTEGRATED PRACTICE APPROACH TO HIV/AIDS PREVENTION

The multiple factors that affect African Americans' response to HIV/AIDS provide support for the position taken by Randolph and

Banks (1993) that a more effective approach to HIV prevention in African American communities (compared to the individually focused behavioral approach) may be to show how HIV prevention relates to one's total life experience or connects to other issues in the community. The integrated practice approach recommended combines multiple methods of intervention–individual, family, group, organization, and community–and proposes a culturally sensitive approach that gives attention to transactions between persons and their environment. The primary target system of the integrated practice approach is the community because community provides context for the sense of connectiveness which is an important part of the African American culture. A person does not acquire HIV alone in a vacuum. Socio-cultural factors influence behaviors, interactions, and transactions. Thus, it is important to focus on the community and how the community can help nurture individual, group, and family behavior such that HIV prevention methods are encouraged. This approach represents a more comprehensive effort to decrease the transmission of HIV among African Americans because it addresses the environment and the situational context experienced by African Americans.

The African American Community

The African American community is the organized collective expression of the African American people in the United States (Billingsley 1992). It is capable of providing resources and assistance through its strengths and in spite of its weaknesses. According to Billingsley (1992) the African American community has an organization, agency, or institution for every conceivable function in the Black community. Billingsley notes that the church, the school, the business enterprise, and voluntary organizations are the four sets of organizations that have been paramount in the African American community throughout history. The community provides an environment of acceptance to African Americans even when mainstream society offers rejection. Given the importance of the community in the lives of African Americans, it is appropriate to utilize community level interventions in addressing the HIV/AIDS epidemic.

The core of the sense of community among African Americans is the recognition of connectiveness shared among people of African descent in America. Billingsley (1992) identifies four aspects in which connectiveness is shared:

> First, geographically, most Black families live in neighbor-hoods where most of their neighbors are also Black. A second sense of community among African-Americans . . . is a shared set of values, which helps to define them. Thirdly, most Black people wherever they live, continue to identify with their heritage to some degree . . . and many who move out . . . or who never lived in one have relatives and friends who have stayed; others return to go to churches, barber shops, and beauty parlors. Finally, there is a set of institutions and organizations which grow out of the African-American heritage identify with it, and serve primarily African-American people and families. (pp. 71-73)

Social workers and health professionals need an understanding of the complexity and strength of community fabric among African Americans in urban and rural areas in order to work effectively in an integrated practice approach with serious community health issues such as AIDS.

Community Practice Around HIV/AIDS Issues

HIV/AIDS is a societal problem that has affected every segment of the population. The pervasiveness of the problem and the devastating affects it has on society have resulted in a number of institutions, organizations, and agencies working to deal with the problem. Some come under public auspices such as social services agencies, public health departments; non-profit auspices such as HIV/AIDS consortiums, education groups, churches; foundations and community-based agencies. Individual workers may also come from a variety of areas–social workers, public health workers, community educators, community activists, church members, and others. This paper focuses on social workers because of the vast array of roles and tasks they are trained to perform in their effort to help people improve their overall well-being and quality of life.

A social worker's involvement in community-based practice with the African American community around issues related to

HIV/AIDS is most likely initiated and sanctioned in one of two ways. The social worker may work for an agency that provides social and/or health services to the community or the worker may be a part of an organization that has funding specifically targeted to work in the area of HIV/AIDS.

The initial level of receptivity the social worker encounters from the community is affected by the agency's or organization's reputation in the community and the professional identification the social worker uses to identify her/his work with the problem. The reputation of the agency or organization in the community, especially as it relates to service delivery and respect for the community, may enhance or hinder the social worker's chances of being openly received by the community. If the overall reputation of the agency or organization is positive or fairly neutral, receptivity of the community to the worker is likely to be greater than if the agency's reputation is not favorable.

Professional identification as indicated by job title also affects the community's response to the social worker. Solomon (1976) suggests that titles which identify the particular nature of problems that the social worker is qualified to address and expected to handle is preferable over the title "social worker." For example, to be identified as a community AIDS specialist, or an AIDS program specialist, is preferable to being identified as a social worker because the designation of social worker in African American communities is often viewed only a little more positively than a "welfare worker" (Solomon, 1976).

Familiarity with the community, its residents, and leaders is needed in order to successfully engage community leaders and gain their support (Kahn, 1994; 1991). It is helpful if the social worker is known by the the community. Assessment of the strengths and specific needs of the community is needed before work can begin.

Assessment of the sense of power in the African American community, especially in relation to HIV/AIDS, is important to the process of engaging the entire community. Talking with a range of community residents, meeting with community leaders, health care workers, and other professionals, and forming several focus groups are ways to gather information about the community's sense of power related to HIV/AIDS. If there is a primary feeling of powerlessness, specific focus needs to be given to enhance motivation levels and instill hope. Gutierrez (1990) summarizes four associated psychological changes presented in the literature that seem crucial for moving individuals from apathy and despair to action:

1. Increasing self-efficacy involves an increase in the belief that one has the ability to produce and to regulate events in one's life.
2. Developing group consciousness involves the development of an awareness of how political structures affect individual and group experiences; it creates a sense of shared fate.
3. Reducing self-blame involves attributing clients problems to the existing power arrangements in society, which free them from feeling responsible for their negative situation.
4. Assuming personal responsibility for change works to help clients become active participants rather than powerless objects (p. 150).

Sharing messages of hope that exist with HIV/AIDS and demonstrating a commitment to work *with* the community in partnership are important strategies for getting the community involved in the HIV prevention effort (Cashman, Fulmer, & Staples, 1994).

Hope for change is more likely when the worker appears to have expertise in the problem area (Solomon, 1976). As a community organizer, the social worker's expertise in work with the African American community will aid in engaging community leaders to endorse and participate in the HIV prevention efforts. Such expertise will be apparent in the worker's use of proper protocol in securing access to the community and its leadership, and in the worker's approach to working in partnership with the community by acknowledging its strengths and established support systems. As a facilitator and educator working with the residents, the worker's expertise about HIV/AIDS generally and in the context of the African American community in particular, will help generate hope that something can be done to improve the problem and its effects on individuals, families, and the community.

The "double consciousness" DuBois (1903) identified in his book, *The Souls of Black Folk,* has forced African Americans to assess carefully all messages to determine both the content of the message and the intent of the messenger. A determination is made early concerning the value of health messages and one's trust in the messenger (Warren, 1992). Thus, the HIV prevention approach discussed in this paper is best implemented with community workers who are: knowledgeable about the African American community; seasoned and comfortable working with and in the African American community; and knowledgeable in the area of HIV/AIDS with cultural sensitivity to African Americans.

COMMUNITY FORUMS AS A STRATEGY FOR EDUCATION AND COMMUNITY BUILDING AROUND HIV/AIDS

Community forums and meetings serve as structures to assemble community residents in order to openly address HIV/AIDS issues in light of their total life experiences and how it connects with their community. If well organized and structured, the forums can provide a relaxed nonjudgmental environment for community residents to share and discuss their experiences and thoughts regarding the HIV/AIDS epidemic and its effect on their life experiences. They can also provide a unique opportunity for education about HIV prevention that is culturally relevant and sensitive to community needs. The following section outlines who should be involved in community forums, how to maximize community participation, where forums should be held, and what topics forums should cover. It should be noted that the strategies discussed in this paper are focused on urban communities because the largest concentration of African Americans are in urban areas (Massey & Denton, 1993). Issues of transportation, location, and the degree of perceived freedom to speak publicly on sensitive topics such as HIV/AIDS can become major barriers to successful use of this model in rural areas or in small towns.

Community Forums: The Groundwork

Key people in the community need to be involved early in the engagement process in order to gain their support and commitment to work toward the overall goal of dealing with the HIV/AIDS epidemic in the community. In addition to support from individuals such as ministers, other religious leaders, bankers, teachers, and some organization leaders, commitment to work on the problem is needed from a wide spectrum of community residents. Such persons may include beauty and barber shop owners, store owners, herbalists, healers indigenous to the African American community, some long-term survivors of HIV, some elders, professionals, paraprofessionals, and others who play an important role in the survival of the community. African Americans' history of self-help, self-reliance, and systematic exclusion from resources available to the wider society has resulted in internal structures and mechanisms of support from which the aforementioned individuals are likely to have gained status and influence in the community. For example, the herbalist and healer may in fact be the primary person to whom community residents go for medical help or treatment (Watson, 1984). Barber and beauty shops are not only places for hair care and personal grooming, they also serve as social gathering places, thus contributing to the status of the owners in the community. Long-term survivors of HIV are important as they can serve as a source of knowledge and hope to those who are already HIV positive.

Wide-spread outreach to community residents needs to focus on HIV/AIDS as a community problem, not as a problem of individuals and/or their families. The stigma of HIV/AIDS in the African American community has been a major barrier to the community's response to the epidemic (Dalton, 1989; Duh, 1991; Gasch, Poulson, Fullilove, & Fullilove, 1991). To help deal with the stigma associated with being infected, having the disease, or having a family member with HIV/AIDS, as well as the stigma attached to the community as a whole, a clear message needs to be sent that an overarching purpose of the forums is to get the community together in an effort to address the problem (HIV/AIDS) collectively and to strengthen the community. Through the use of forums the community can: talk openly, discuss their concerns, and learn about HIV/AIDS and its effects on the community; develop strategies to address what can be done about the effects of the epidemic on the community; learn and discuss what can be done as a community, not just as individuals, to prevent the spread of HIV; and learn about resources available to deal with the epidemic. Thus, a major focus of the forums is education.

The message which informs the community of the forums needs to foster hope that indeed measures can be taken to deal with the epidemic. It also needs to be clear that the prevention effort is developed and conducted in partnership with the community. Cashman, Fulmer and Staples (1994) emphasize the importance of working in partnership with the community to get increased community participation. A key strategy to strengthen community participation is the early development of an advisory committee composed of some key people in the community. Such a group can help insure that the development and implementation of the forums reflect the partnership with the community and encourage collaboration and participation in every phase of the process. The advisory committee may be especially helpful with suggestions on specific outreach strategies to reach various segments of the community residents.

The location of the forums and meetings are key to their success. Meetings should be held at various sites throughout the community in order to enhance the comfortability and convenience of participants. For example, some forums or meetings may be held at the local beauty or barber shops, at churches, in senior centers, at the local recreation centers or any number of places accessible, comfortable, and/or familiar to community residents. Failure, negative valuation, and boredom experienced by many African Americans in formal educational settings have resulted in resistance from many to participate in activities held in settings that physically resemble and present information through formats frequently used in many public schools (Solomon, 1976).

Topics for the forums and meetings will vary according to the needs of community residents. Sessions must be geared toward the overall goal of relating HIV prevention to the situational and environmental context and realities of their lives. The interrelatedness of the effects of HIV/AIDS on the entire African American community must be stressed. It is important that it is made clear that the forums are not just for those who have the virus, are at high risk, or have the disease. Therefore, it is crucial that close collaboration between the community and others involved is utilized to develop effective strategies to introduce the community to the prevention program. Topics discussed in each session need to address issues and problems related to HIV and AIDS in relation to the community as a unit, and across the age spectrum in order to maintain involvement of all segments of the community, both young and old.

The range of issues for discussion at the forums may vary depending on the needs of the neighborhood or community. Some issues to be discussed include: African Americans' beliefs and feelings about HIV and AIDS; the origin of the disease; beliefs about conspiracy and genocide related to the virus; homosexuality and bisexuality in the African American community; heterosexual relationships among African Americans; drugs in the community and drug use; poverty, unemployment, violence, crime, and poor health; the effects of AIDS on the nuclear and extended family system; HIV/AIDS and the elderly; religious institutions and their response to the AIDS epidemic; spirituality and spiritual needs; the increased rate of AIDS among African American women and children; HIV transmission and AIDS among adolescents; and their thoughts and feelings about the effectiveness of HIV/AIDS prevention. Discussion on such issues in community forums provides residents in African American communities with a structure to openly discuss issues that are vital to them in an environment where they can be heard, where information is provided that acknowledges their realities, and where specific steps are shared that may affect their lives positively.

A social worker trained in group process techniques can provide skilled facilitation of the forums. This will assure that group process takes place in a meaningful way. At the beginning of each forum, the purpose of the session should be clearly stated and general ground rules presented. The facilitator needs to assure that a variety of people are given the opportunity to speak. It is important that the participants know that their concerns are important and will be heard in a nonthreatening environment. Verbal participation is strictly voluntary. Before the end of each session, a summary of the session and recommendations generated during the session need to be presented. Persons knowledgeable about HIV/AIDS and the African American community need to be present at each session to provide accurate information to questions or misinformation, and to share information, especially regarding HIV prevention.

It may be necessary at times to have forums and meetings which are not open to all in the community but are targeted to specific subgroups within the community. Some forums or meetings may need to be for women only, men only, teens only, or IVDUers only. For example, Lockett (1990) suggests that prostitutes may be excellent AIDS prevention educators and resources to African American women in helping them understand how to protect themselves and how to get their male partners to wear condoms. Small group sessions may be needed occasionally around specifics such as supporting women to implement techniques for negotiating condom use with a partner. Older residents may have special concerns around issues of caregiving to infected children and becoming surrogate parents to their grandchildren, as well as potential risk of transmission of the virus to themselves and/or their grandchildren.

Continued supportive involvement of key leaders is essential. HIV/AIDS has not been a topic of open constructive discussion in the African American community. The development and/or maintenance of a community environment that supports HIV prevention and fosters support for those infected with the virus, persons with AIDS (PWAs), and their families is important. Key people in the community can play a major role in bringing HIV/AIDS "out of the closet" by publicly supporting HIV prevention efforts. It is important that social workers working with key community people continue to encourage them to actively reinforce support for the HIV prevention efforts.

Strengthening linkages between the community groups and those who have established programs, services, and resources for HIV prevention and AIDS treatment in the community is an important role for the social worker. The proposed approach to HIV prevention views work with existing programs as important to maximize resources and to help make existing programs more relevant and effective to African Americans.

BENEFITS OF AN INTEGRATED APPROACH TO HIV/AIDS PREVENTION

Work with the community as a primary target of intervention in HIV/AIDS prevention efforts rather than the individual has potential benefits for individuals and the community. The approach described in this paper allows individuals the opportunity to integrate individual focused risk reduction behavior change messages into their total life experiences. This process makes messages more relevant and increases the chances of adherence to some behavioral changes related to HIV prevention. Engaging a broad spectrum of leaders and citizens to work together on an issue of importance to the community promotes interaction among community residents and opens avenues for future work on other projects of concern to the community.

Open forums are useful mechanisms to help bring the community together to discuss issues relevant to the community and its residents. Community residents coming together to learn and have input on issues that are important to them related to HIV/AIDS brings about more social interaction and may nurture a stronger sense of community at the local level (Rohe & Gates, 1985).

A major purpose of the forums and meetings is to nurture a sense of community in an environment that is historically and culturally familiar to African Americans. Richards (1990) notes that when the life of the group is threatened, ritual is used to strengthen its members psychologically and emotionally by creating a sense of order that will better enable them to deal with their problems in a constructive way. She describes ritual as a communal participatory process:

> We "testified," speaking on the day's or the week's experience. We shared the pain of those experiences and received from the group affirmations of our existence as suffering beings. As we "laid down our burdens" we became lighter. As we testified and listened to others testify, we began to understand ourselves as communal beings, no longer the kind of person that the slave system tried to make of us. Through rituals we again became a community. (p. 217)

Thus the forums and meetings are not only designed to address specific issues of HIV prevention but to also provide a mechanism to help foster hope and exercise a spirit of expression and reaffimation. As no mandatory requirements are attached to residents' participation, attendance indicates interest in giving and/or receiving information. Opportunities for such to happen must be maximized by the facilitator/educator in order to nurture continued involvement of the residents in the community's fight against AIDS.

The structure of open forums reduces the stigma attached to participating in HIV/AIDS prevention efforts either as the deliverer or receiver of prevention. Persons are free to attend and participate as members of the community, not as individuals seeking help. The forums also provide opportunities for residents of the community to speak and be heard in a structured environment, participate in discussions, and get feedback on their thoughts and concerns about HIV/AIDS. The forums allow those who already have established HIV/AIDS programs in the commmunity to learn more about the residents and to strengthen their programs in efforts to serve African Americans more effectively.

The proposed integrated practice approach also provides an opportunity for the church to become more actively involved with the problem of HIV/AIDS without being the primary initiator at the outset. The church is a powerful influence with resources in African American communities. It can be an important source of support for HIV prevention efforts and support services; however, it has not been very active regarding HIV/AIDS. In 1988, the National Black Church Consortium on Critical Health Care Needs issued an official statement calling for an immediate response to the AIDS epidemic, but at the local level the response appears to have been given low priority (Jonsen & Stryker, 1993). Owens (1995) interviewed 14 African American ministers throughout New Jersey regarding their churches' response to AIDS. She reports that all the ministers recognized a need for the church's involvement in the fight against AIDS and had specific suggestions of how the church could be helpful; however, none of the fourteen churches were actively involved in providing services specific to HIV/AIDS. Although a convenient sample was used in this study, this finding is disturbing in light of the fact that AIDS is the leading cause of death in New Jersey for African American women between the ages of 15-44 and ranks fifth in the nation in reported AIDS cases (New Jersey Women and AIDS Network, 1994).

Billingsley (1992) interviewed 71 churches along the Eastern Seaboard to document Black churches' responses to current social conditions. He cites two African American churches in Maryland, a small church and a 500 member middle class church, St. John Baptist Church, for their leadership role in expanding education efforts in the fight against AIDS among African Americans. The small church took leadership in organizing other African American churches to expand AIDS education and St. John Baptist Church put into operation an AIDS education program for the African American community (Billingsley, 1992). The program recruits volunteers from the church and trains them to teach AIDS education and provide counseling to affected patients. Plans are to conduct seminars in twenty-five African American churches in addition to conducting regular seminars on AIDS for community leaders and professionals (Billingsley, 1992).

The nature of HIV and its modes of transmission make it a problem that the church does not readily embrace. Although activity regarding HIV/AIDS has been slow, Dalton (1989) states that when we look at the Black church historically, it has time and again demonstrated its awareness of the variability and fragility of human existence and has responded to the spiritual and nonspiritual needs of the community. The involvement of the church in the integrated community based practice approach may allow church members and leaders to learn more about the virus and disease in the context of the community residents' lives. Involvement of church leaders and members may help some reluctant community residents to see the church in a more favorable light in relation to its concern about HIV/AIDS and the disease's effect on their lives.

Finally, organizing and working with the African American community around HIV/AIDS issues may help the community to maintain and perhaps broaden relationships and structures to work on other issues that are pressing for the community. HIV/AIDS affects so many aspects of African Americans' lives that dealing with the problem certainly means dealing with many factors that affect their lives and their community. Linkages established as a result of working together on HIV prevention may motivate some community leaders and residents to work together on other issues that affect their community.

REFERENCES

Beardsley, E. H. (1990). Race as a factor in health. In R. D. Apple (Ed.), *Women health and medicine in America* (pp. 121-140). New Brunswick, NJ: Rutgers University Press.

Becker, M. H., & Joseph, J. (1988). AIDS and behavioral change to reduce risk: A review. *American Journal of Public Health, 78,* 394-410.

Billingsley, A. (1992). *Climbing Jacob's ladder.* New York: Simon & Schuster.

Cashman, S. B., Fulmer, H. S, & Staples, L. (1994). Community health: Beyond care for individuals. *Social Policy, 24*(4), 52-62.

Centers for Disease Control and Prevention (June 1994). *HIV/AIDS surveillance report, 6*(1). Atlanta, GA: Centers for Disease Control and Prevention.

Centers for Disease Control and Prevention (November, 1993a). Facts about HIV/AIDS and race/ethnicity. *HIV/AIDS Prevention.* Atlanta, GA: Centers for Disease Control and Prevention.

Centers for Disease Control and Prevention (October, 1993b). Facts about women and HIV/AIDS. *HIV/AIDS Prevention.* Atlanta, GA: Centers for Disease Control and Prevention.

Cummings, S. (1969). Family socialization and fatalism among Black adolescents. *Journal of Social Issues, 25,* 13-27.

Dalton, H. L. (1989). AIDS in Blackface. *Daedalus, 118,* 205-227.

DuBois, W. E. B. (1903). *The souls of Black folk.* Chicago: McClurg.

Duh, S.V. (1991). *Blacks and aids: Causes and origins.* Newberry Park, CA: Sage Publications, Inc.

Gasch, H., Poulson, M., Fullilove, R.E., & Fullilove, M.T. (1991). Shaping AIDS education and prevention programs for African Americans amidst community decline. *Journal of Negro Education, 60*(1), pp. 85-96.

Gutierrez, L. (1990). Working with women of color: An empowerment perspective. *Social Work, 35*(2), 149-153.

Jackson, J. J. (1981). Urban Black American. In A. Harwood (Ed.), *Ethnicity and medical care* (pp. 37-129). Cambridge, MA: Harvard University Press.

Jaynes, G.D. & Williams, R. M., Jr. (Eds.) (1989). Black American's health. *A common destiny: Blacks and American society.* Washington, DC: National Academy Press.

Jenkins, B., Lamar, V. L., Thompson-Crumble J. (1993). AIDS among African Americans: A social epidemic. *The Journal of Black Psychology, 19*(2), 108-122.

Jonsen, A. R. & Stryker, J. (eds) (1993). *The social impact of AIDS in the United States.* Washington, D.C.: National Academy Press.

Kahn, S. (1994). *How people get power.* Washington, DC: NASW Press.

Kahn, S. (1991). *Organizing: A guide for grassroots leaders.* Washington, DC: NASW Press.

Kirp, D. L. & Bayer, R. (July 1993). Needles and race. *The Atlantic, 272*(1), 38-442.

Lockett, G. (1990). Black prostitutes and AIDS. In E.C. White (Ed.), *The Black women's health book: Speaking for ourselves.* Seattle, WA: Seal Press, 182-186.

Massey, D. S. & Denton, N. A. (1993). *American Apartheid: Segregation and the making of the underclass.* Cambridge, MA: Harvard University Press.

National Center for Health Statistics. (1994). *Health, United States, 1993* (DHHS Pub. No. (PHS) 94-1232). Hyattsville, MD: Public Health Service.

New Jersey Women and AIDS Network, (1994). *Facts about women and AIDS.* New Brunswick, NJ: Author.

Owens, S. (1995). *Where does the Black church stand on AIDS.* Manuscript submitted for publication.

Quimby, E. (1993). Obstacles to reducing AIDS among African Americans. *The Journal of Black Psychology, 19*(2), 215-221.

Randolph, S. M. & Banks, H. D. (1993). Making a way out of no way: The promise of Africentric approaches to HIV prevention. *The Journal of Black Psychology, 19*(2), 204-214.

Richards, D. (1990). The implications of African American spirituality. In M. K. Asante & K.W. Asante (Eds.), *African culture: The rhythms of unity* (pp. 207-231). NJ: Africa World Press, Inc.

Richie, B. (1990). AIDS: In living color. In E. C. White (Ed.), *The Black women's health book: Speaking for ourselves* (pp. 182-186). Seattle, WA: Seal Press.

Rohe, W. M. & Gates, L. B. (1985). *Planning with neighborhoods.* Chapel Hill, N.C: The University of North Carolina Press.

Solomon, B. B. (1976). *Black empowerment: Social work in oppressed communities.* New York: Columbia University Press.

Thomas, S. B., & Quinn, S. C. (1991). Public health then and now. *American Journal of Public Health, 81*(11), 1498-1505.

U.S. Department of Health and Human Services (1985). *Report of the Secretary's Task Force on Black and Minority Health.* Washington, DC: U.S. Government Printing Office.

Villarosa, L. (Ed.), (1994). *Body and soul.* New York: Harper Collins Publishers, Inc.

Warren, R. C. (1992). Health education and Black health status. In R. L. Braithwaite & S. E. Taylor (Eds.), *Health issues in the Black community* (pp. 241-254). CA: Jossey-Bass.

Watson, W. H. (Ed.), (1984). *Black folk medicine: The therapeutic significance of faith and trust.* New Brunswick: Transaction Books.

Redirecting the Lives of Urban Black Males: An Assessment of Milwaukee's Midnight Basketball League

Walter C. Farrell, Jr., PhD, MSPH
James H. Johnson, Jr., PhD
Marty Sapp, EdD
Roger M. Pumphrey, DMin
Shirley Freeman, EdD

SUMMARY. Midnight Basketball is one example of a new generation of social resource programs which are designed to mend the

Walter Farrell, Jr., is Professor in the Department of Educational Policy and
Community Studies and the Graduate Program in Urban Studies at the University
of Wisconsin-Milwaukee.

James Johnson, Jr., is E. Maynard Adams Professor of Geography, Sociology,
and the Kenan-Flagler Business School at the University of North Carolina at
Chapel Hill.

Marty Sapp is Associate Professor in the Department of Educational Psychology at the University of Wisconsin-Milwaukee.

Roger M. Pumphrey is a teacher at the Kilmer Alternative School of the
Milwaukee Public Schools.

Shirley Freeman is Associate Professor in the Department of Curriculum and
Instruction at the University of Arkansas at Little Rock.

Address correspondence to: Walter C. Farrell, Jr., Professor, Department of
Educational Policy and Community Studies, Enderis Hall #521, University of
Wisconsin-Milwaukee, Milwaukee, WI 53201.

[Haworth co-indexing entry note]: "Redirecting the Lives of Urban Black Males: An Assessment of
Milwaukee's Midnight Basketball League." Farrell, Walter C., Jr. et al. Co-published simultaneously in
Journal of Community Practice (The Haworth Press, Inc.) Vol. 2, No. 4, 1995, pp. 91-107; and: *African
American Community Practice Models: Historical and Contemporary Responses* (ed: Iris Carlton-LaNey,
and N. Yolanda Burwell) The Haworth Press, Inc., 1996, pp. 91-107. Single or multiple copies of this article
are available from The Haworth Document Delivery Service [1-800-342-9678, 9:00 a.m. - 5:00 p.m. (EST)].

91

social fabric of inner city communities. In this paper, we present the results of an evaluation of Milwaukee's Midnight Basketball League, *In the Paint at One Two,* which indicates that the "returns" on the money invested in the program are far greater than the returns on the enormously popular punitive and paternalistic policies and programs currently advocated at all levels of government. During the first year, the Midnight Basketball program (1) reduced crime rates by 30% in the target area, (2) created a safe haven in which participants (and the fans) could engage in positive social activities, (3) channeled the energy of gang members in a positive direction, and (4) significantly improved the educational and career aspirations of program participants. Nearly all of the participants indicate that such leagues should be developed throughout the city of Milwaukee. *[Article copies available from The Haworth Document Delivery Service: 1-800-342-9678.]*

KEYWORDS. Inner city, midnight basketball, recreation, urban black males, urban crime, urban policy, urban violence

There is a contemporary trend in U.S. cities in which a recreational activity, "midnight basketball," is captivating inner-city youth. G. Van Standifer, an African American male, founded the Midnight Basketball League in Glenarden, Maryland in June 1986, as a summer program to keep high risk young men–principally high school dropouts who usually were unemployed–off the streets. However, the purpose of the program, as envisioned by its founder, was not simply to teach youths how to play basketball. Rather, by scheduling the games between 12 a.m. and 3 a.m., when many gang-and drug-related crimes occur, a major goal was to reduce the incidence of lethal violence in inner-city communities. The program also included activities designed to foster responsibility in all walks of adult life. For example, the program encouraged those males who had fathered children outside of marriage to assume responsibility for their offspring (Collins & Cohen, 1993; "New Book," 1993; Will, 1990).

Since its launching in Glenarden, Maryland in 1986, the Midnight Basketball League has spread to a number of U.S. cities, including Chicago, Illinois; Philadelphia, Pennsylvania; Little Rock, Arkansas; Phoenix, Arizona; and Milwaukee, Wisconsin. The fact that police and leaders of inner-city community-based recreational programs believe the league promotes discipline and reduces alcohol and drug abuse, crime, and antisocial behavior of male youth at a variety of ages is one of the major forces influencing its diffusion throughout urban America (Bessone, 1992; Cooper, 1994; Midnight Basketball, 1994; Tenille, 1994). Among the cities in which Midnight Basketball Leagues have been established, the Chicago program has received the most media attention, which encouraged other cities to begin their programs (Bessone, 1992; Freking, 1992; Laningham, 1991; Walker, 1991a, 1991b).

In February 1990, *The New York Times* reported that there were approximately 110 gangs in Chicago and that the Chicago Housing Authority (CHA) was using the Midnight Basketball League as a new urban strategy to reduce crime and convert gang members. Funded by a $25,000 federal grant and other resources, the program was launched on Chicago's west side, with the initial organizing session held at Malcolm X College on February 6, 1990. Thirty-two teams, each comprised of ten inner-city young males between the ages of 18 and 24, signed up to participate in Chicago's Midnight Basketball League. The teams were given names such as the Bulls and the Lakers, and a four month season was established, with games scheduled on Tuesdays and Thursdays, from 10 p.m. to 2 a.m., at the Horner and Rockwell Projects (Curry, 1990).

The Chicago police are present at all times during practice and the playing of games, and players are not allowed to wear any insignia that identifies them as gang members. The rules are strict; if a player is caught using drugs or fighting, he will be suspended and faces possible banishment. Practice occurs from 8 p.m. to midnight. Any players absent are not able to play in the next game. Basketball is used as a hook to assist these young males in securing a high school diploma, getting a job, and learning family development skills. The players receive fringe benefits such as tokens to attend games, haircuts, and drug and job counseling. After the League was launched, police reported that gang killings decreased in Chicago during the late night and early morning hours (Bessone, 1992; Curry, 1990; "In a Late," 1989).

In this paper, we report the results of an evaluation of the Midnight Basketball League (*In the Paint at One Two*) in Milwaukee, Wisconsin. This is the first comprehensive assessment of any of these programs. Whereas previous observers have primarily highlighted the impact of such programs on crime rates, the focus in this paper is on the broader perceptions and experiences of participants in the Milwaukee program.

THE MILWAUKEE CONTEXT

Today, African American youth–especially in urban areas–are experiencing an extremely difficult period of adjustment to a rapidly changing local, national, and global economy. They are being negatively impacted by a wide range of social and economic factors that make it difficult for them to finish school, to build strong families, and simply to survive. These factors are particularly severe in urban areas where most African Americans reside, and they are especially acute for large numbers of Blacks in Milwaukee. Even as the Black middle class has doubled over the past quarter century, the social, economic, and occupational situations of all other Blacks have worsened or have remained the same. African Americans not only continue to lag behind Whites in these categories, but even more disturbing, is the expanding gulf between the haves and the have-nots in the Black community (Farrell & Johnson, 1992).

A growing number of African American youth suffer from a deeply held and growing sense of hopelessness, and from a belief that they cannot succeed as individuals, students, or family members. They feel they have no chance to make it in the present or the future and that they have no control over or input into those factors that will determine the outcome of their lives. As a consequence, poor inner-city youth frequently engage in behaviors that are in stark opposition to the tenets of mainstream society as they attempt to valorize notions of affirmation and resistance to their marginal socioeconomic conditions (Lott, 1992, p. 72). Any casual examination of urban Black communities anywhere in this nation will provide a firm basis for this pervasive lack of hope.

In Milwaukee, as in most other large U.S. cities, there is a socially and geographically distinct Black community. It is largely located on the northside of the city and is comprised of some 48 census tracts where Blacks constitute the majority of the residents. This area is made up of neighborhoods that are isolated socially and marginalized economically from the mainstream of the Milwaukee society, as evidenced by the following statistics:

- More than two-thirds of all Black Milwaukeeans live in these census tracts. Substantial numbers of the residents are poor, 40% or more in most instances, representing one of the highest concentrations of poverty in a major U.S. metropolitan area during the 1980s (Schultze, 1993).
- More than a third of all Black families in these neighborhoods are headed by females–the highest concentration in the city. The overwhelming preponderance of these female-headed households contain children and are engulfed by poverty (Farrell & Johnson, 1992).
- Only a modest number of families in these neighborhoods have a median family income above $10,000 per year, and the majority of households are larger than four persons. Taken together, median income and household size, the community's economic base is substantially below the $13,000 level the U.S. Department of Labor has designated as being sufficient to lift an urban family of four above the poverty level (Farrell & Johnson, 1992).
- Adult education levels in these neighborhoods, as measured by high school graduation, are among the lowest in the city. And when one examines the educational skills of many of those who have graduated, the picture is even more dismal (Farrell & Johnson, 1992).
- Unemployment in the area is more than double that anywhere else in Milwaukee, and for Black males, it is worst of all. A study of the labor market experiences of young African American men, ages 20-24, from January 1988 through March 1991, revealed an average unemployment rate of 40%, more than ten times the rate of their majority counterparts. Moreover, those who were employed were largely relegated to marginal, low-wage jobs (Rose, Edari, Quinn, & Pawasarat, 1992).

Collectively, these stark realities narrow aspirations and opportunities and re-enforce hopelessness. Children and teens in Milwaukee's socioeconomically distressed neighborhoods, especially males, frequently lack access to positive social and recreational outlets; therefore, they are easily recruited by their peers, and others, into gang and/or gang-related antisocial activities. This pattern of development is reflected in the increase in gang membership, in juvenile arrests for murder and other crimes, and in the escalating rate of juvenile and young adult incarceration ("Children No More," 1992). This is the context that stimulated the midnight basketball initiative which is designed to provide recreational opportunities and life skills development for inner-city males who are at risk of being overwhelmed by a socially and economically adverse environment (Farrell & Johnson, 1992).

Milwaukee's Midnight Basketball League

Milwaukee's Midnight Basketball League (*In the Paint at One Two*) began operation on July 6, 1992 at the Hillside Unit of the Milwaukee Boys' and Girls' Club.

Founded by businessman Jerry Lestina, President of Roundy's Foods, one of Wisconsin's largest corporations, *it is entirely funded by the private sector.* Originally comprised of 16 teams located in Milwaukee's northside predominantly Black community, games are played three nights a week (Monday, Tuesday, and Wednesday) from July through the first week of September. (An additional league of eight teams was established in Milwaukee's Southside, low-income community in 1993, serving a predominantly Hispanic and White male population.) *In the Paint at One Two,* like other Midnight Basketball Leagues throughout the nation, was designed to serve as an alternative to drugs, gangs, and violence for young adult males in the inner-city of Milwaukee.

As in other programs around the country, players are required to meet with mentors/speakers for one-half hour after every game to discuss their career, educational, and life aspirations. More than 100 mentors/speakers—men and women—from government, the corporate sector, law enforcement, community-based organizations, public education, the university, and the clergy participated in these sessions. They focused on job skills, drug abuse, and life skills, and assisted the midnight basketball participants in taking stock of where they are and in charting a new direction for their futures. The evaluation results, presented below, provide critical insights into the impacts of these and other program activities on the lives of the participants in Milwaukee's Midnight Basketball League.

RESEARCH DESIGN

Participants in the League were surveyed with an instrument developed by a committee comprised of members of the League's board of directors, social science researchers, a police official, a youth-serving community-based organization executive, corporate leaders, and marketing researchers. Survey statements were pre-tested with members of the Ford Foundation's 1992 Summer Youth Commission on Urban Poverty, based in Durham, North Carolina (and area residents), to ensure clarity, reliability, and validity. The Youth Commission and the related population are reflective of the racial and socioeconomic backgrounds of the Midnight Basketball League participants.

The first section of the survey was designed to collect information on participants' personal background (e.g., employment status, annual income, school status, marital status, number of children, and attitudes toward Milwaukee). Section two solicited data on participants' *perceptions and experiences (e.g., educational and career opportunities, safety/security, crime, gangs, home issues, alcohol and drugs, recreational opportunities, and overall views of the midnight basketball league).* In the latter section, each participant was asked to place an (X) in the box under one of the five categories adjacent to the statements: *(1) Strongly Disagree [SD], (2) Disagree [D], (3) No Opinion [NO], (4) Agree [A], and (5) Strongly Agree [SA].*

The evaluation survey was administered to a 60% sample (96/160) of league participants. Although it was not randomly derived, the sample—because of its size—was representative of the personal and social backgrounds as well as the perceptions and experiences of league players. Coaches and/or mentors/speakers, after being given instructions by a member of the evaluation team, administered the evaluation survey instruments at the end of League games during the last three days of 1992-93 season. These findings are limited to the participants in Milwaukee's Midnight Basketball League and are thus generalizable to that population. However, they have implications for other African American males of a similar demographic profile in urban areas throughout the nation.

RESULTS

Ninety-six of the midnight basketball players were surveyed across the 16 teams. Not all participants answered all statements; therefore, the number (N) of participants per statement ranges from a low of 64 to a high of 92. The percentage response was rounded to the nearest tenth, resulting in a total percentage slightly below or slightly above 100% in some instances. The demographic characteristics of the participants are summarized below, followed by an assessment of their perceptions of and experiences in the Midnight Basketball League.

Demographic Characteristics

All of the participants in the Milwaukee Midnight Basketball League are African American males between the ages of 18 and 25. Nearly all are single (93%); 6% are married, and 1% divorced. Despite the low marriage rate, over half have children (30% have fathered two or more children), and 22% have at least one child.

The level of educational attainment for this group is substantially higher than the average years of schooling for Black males in that age group (18-25) in the City of Milwaukee based on the 1990 Census. Ninety-two percent of the participants are high school graduates, and 14% are college graduates.

Despite above-average education levels, the group's unemployment rate (42%) is consistent with that of Milwaukee's inner-city African American male population. Only 58% of the participants are employed, and among this group, only 53% work full time. The rest (47%) work part-time and usually work 25 hours or less per week.

Reflective of their marginal status in the Milwaukee labor market, only 19% of the participants who work reported earnings in excess of $15,000 per year. The majority earned substantially less–59% less than $10,000 and 30% less than $5,000 annually.

Notwithstanding their economically meager existence, nearly three-fourths (74%) of the participants indicate that they like living in Milwaukee. When asked why they like living in the city, most (68%) give family-related reasons. Among those expressing a dislike for living in Milwaukee, lack of jobs/job prospects (52%) and other quality of life factors are the dominant reasons given.

Perceptions and Experiences

A majority of the participants believe that the midnight basketball is a success (83%) and express pride in being involved in the program (86%). More than four-fifths (81%) of the participants believe that the league's tone of positive values (i.e., high moral standards, high expectations, and positive messages) is realistic (Table 1).

Most of the participants (71%) view the experience as more than an opportunity to play basketball. Among the other benefits, the participants note the following: They report forming friendships (81%) and trusting (73%) and respectful (88%) relationships with their coaches and teammates as well as with other players in the program. *This level of respect among this age group of Black males is significant in that this is the group among which a disproportionate amount of Black-on-Black violent crime occurs* (Table 1).

Most of the participants in Milwaukee's Midnight Basketball League indicate that the program helps them to clarify their educational goals and career aspirations. In the evaluation survey, more than three-fourths express an interest in pursuing additional education (Table 2). Sixty-nine percent indicate that they want to earn an associate degree or higher, and 45% plan to earn a bachelor's degree or higher. They (78%) note that the speaker/mentor sessions (which occur after each game and are one-half hour in length) are especially instrumental in heightening their educational and career aspirations. To date, more than $15,000 in scholarships have been awarded to league players to enable them to pursue postsecondary education in proprietary/trade schools, community and technical colleges, four-year colleges and universities, and graduate schools (Burkee, 1994). Seventy-nine percent of the participants express the feeling that the mentors/speakers are truly concerned about them as individuals, and 78% said that they identify with their messages (Table 2).

In addition to improving their educational and career aspirations, the Midnight Basketball League appears to have reduced stress in the lives of the participants, especially in their home environments,

TABLE 1. ITP Participants' Views of In the Paint at One Two

Issues	% SD	D	NO	A	SA
1. ITP* is a success (n = 80)	1.3	2.5	13.8	17.5	65.0
2. Proud to be involved in ITP (n = 78)	–	–	14.1	15.4	70.5
3. Tone of ITP . . . moral standards, high expectations, positive messages is realistic (n = 80)	–	2.1	16.3	27.5	53.8
4. ITP means more than basketball (n = 80)	–	2.5	26.3	30.0	41.3
5. Formed friendships with ITP members (n = 80)	–	2.5	16.3	30.0	51.3
6. Feel I can trust ITP participants (n = 81)	2.5	7.4	17.3	46.9	25.9
7. Respect all other participants (n = 81)	–	1.2	11.1	54.3	33.3
8. Get along with teammates and coach (n = 81)	1.2	1.2	16.0	39.5	42.0
9. Feel physically safe in gym (n = 80)	–	2.5	20.0	38.8	38.8
10. ITP rules are reasonable (n = 78)	2.6	2.6	20.5	46.2	28.2
11. Consequences for violating ITP rules are fair . . . applied consistently (n = 80)	1.3	7.5	16.3	43.8	31.3
12. Game rules are fair (n = 80)	2.5	6.3	18.8	40.0	32.5
13. Mentor/speaker sessions are valuable (n = 81)	2.5	1.2	17.3	48.1	30.9
14. Can relate to issues mentors/speakers addressing (n = 81)	–	3.7	18.5	37.0	40.7
15. Mentors/speakers are concerned about me and players (n = 81)	2.5	4.9	25.9	38.3	28.4
16. Plan to continue participation in ITP (n = 81)	1.2	3.7	14.8	23.5	56.8

*In the Paint at One Two (Midnight Basketball League).

and to have encouraged them to avoid crime. Forty-two percent indicate that the Midnight Basketball League has helped to improve their home situations (Table 3), and more than two-thirds believe that the program has encouraged them, individually, to avoid crime (Table 4). Eighty-two percent report that they have not been involved in any criminal activity during their participation in the Midnight Basketball League. Only 11% acknowledge involvement

TABLE 2. ITP Participants' Perceptions of Educational/Career Opportunities

Issues	% SD	D	NO	A	SA
1. Expect ITP* to Assist Ed. Aspirations (n = 86)	1.2	5.8	33.7	39.5	19.8
2. Experience stimulated career interest (n = 84)	2.4	2.4	27.4	41.7	26.2
3. ITP mentor/speaker sessions have helped (n = 85)	5.9	5.9	20.0	43.5	24.7

*In the Paint at One Two (Midnight Basketball League).

TABLE 3. ITP Participants' Perceptions of Home Issues

Issues	% SD	D	NO	A	SA
1. Home situation improved during ITP* participation (n = 83)	3.6	12.0	42.2	20.5	21.7
2. Current home situation not good (n = 82)	31.7	17.1	23.2	6.1	22.0

*In the Paint at One Two (Midnight Basketball League).

TABLE 4. ITP Participants' Perceptions of Crime

Issues	% SD	D	NO	A	SA
1. ITP* is helping prevent crime (n = 83)	6.0	3.6	25.3	38.6	26.5
2. More midnight basketball leagues will help prevent crime in city (n = 86)	3.5	1.2	10.5	25.6	59.3
3. Not involved in criminal activity since involved in ITP (n = 84)	7.1	3.6	7.1	8.3	73.8
4. ITP has encouraged me to avoid crime (n = 83)	2.4	6.0	24.1	41.0	26.5

*In the Paint at One Two (Midnight Basketball League).

in such activity, and program records indicate that the offenses are minor (Table 4).

Also, nearly two-thirds (65%) of the participants believe that Midnight Basketball is helping to prevent crime in the Hillside community where the games are played (Table 4). Seventy-eight percent indicate that they feel safe in the gymnasium and on the grounds of the facility (Tables 1 and 5), and 74% observed that the community in which the games are played is safe (Table 5). Participants express the view that the Hillside community, as a consequence of the league, is much safer than their own communities. *In addition, a large percentage (85%) of the participants believe that more such programs would help to prevent crime throughout the city* (Table 4).

What were the participants' overall evaluations of Milwaukee's Midnight Basketball League? Seventy-eight percent of the participants believe that Midnight Basketball is a much-needed recreational outlet for young Black men. Approximately two-thirds of the participants believe that it has contributed to a reduction in crime, gang activity, and violence on game nights (Table 6), and 60% feel that gang members respect the Midnight Basketball League and thus do not engage in negative behavior when in attendance at league games (Table 7).

The program is consistently viewed as positive across all categories of response. Four-fifths of the participants indicate that such leagues should be developed throughout the City of Milwaukee, and more than three-fourths indicate that Midnight Basketball is much more than a recreational program, that it is a program that prepares one for life (Table 6).

DISCUSSION AND CONCLUSIONS

Over the past three decades, Milwaukee and other U.S. cities have been plagued by rising rates of concentrated and persistent

TABLE 5. ITP Participants' Perceptions of Safety/Security

Issues	% SD	D	NO	A	SA
1. Community in which ITP* plays is safe (n = 86)	−	8.1	17.4	38.4	36.0
2. Live in safe community (n = 85)	8.2	15.3	11.8	40.0	24.7
3. ITP has made community safer during game nights (n = 88)	2.3	2.3	10.2	47.7	37.5

*In the Paint at One Two (Midnight Basketball League).

TABLE 6. ITP Participants' Perceptions of Recreational Opportunities for Inner-City Youth

Issues	% SD	D	NO	A	SA
1. Current inner-city youth recreational opportunities inadequate (n = 80)	6.3	5.0	15.0	16.3	57.5
2. Current inner-city youth recreational opportunities adequate (n = 80)	12.5	28.8	21.3	16.3	21.3
3. ITP* is needed recreational outlet for young men (n = 78)	1.3	3.8	16.7	11.5	66.7
4. Believe ITP has caused reduction in crime, gang activity, and violence during game nights (n = 79)	10.1	6.3	17.0	22.8	41.8
5. ITP programs should be developed throughout Milwaukee (n = 80)	—	2.3	18.8	15.0	65.0
6. ITP is more than recreation . . . career guidance, self-development, preparation for life (n = 79)	—	2.5	21.5	25.3	50.6

*In the Paint at One Two (Midnight Basketball League).

TABLE 7. ITP Participants' Perceptions of Gang Activity at ITP Games

Issues	% SD	D	NO	A	SA
1. ITP* games are gang controlled (n = 84)	29.8	8.3	27.4	13.1	21.4
2. Gang members respect ITP games, no negative behavior (n = 86)	5.8	4.7	29.1	29.1	31.4
3. Gang activity decreased during ITP game night (n = 84)	4.8	6.0	44.0	20.2	25.0

*In the Paint at One Two (Midnight Basketball League).

poverty, joblessness, family disruption, out-of-wedlock births, and gang-and drug-related lethal violence. Despite the wide range of theories that exist regarding the forces responsible for the steadily deteriorating quality of life in inner-city communities, *one perspective on these problems has held sway in public policy circles over the last two decades: that a deterioration in individual responsibility and family morals and values, rooted in liberal social welfare policies and programs of the 1960s, is the primary causal agent.*

Nonetheless, Bluestone, Stevenson, and Tilley (1992) have documented the increasing joblessness of Black males in comparison to their White counterparts even when age and education were controlled. During the 1980s, according to their study, the jobless rate for 20 year old Black men (21.6%) was almost five times higher than the rate for their White counterparts (4.8%). For those Black males with less than a high school education, the disparity was even greater.

Moreover, their findings suggest that, over the last 20 years, race-based discrimination has been increasing rather than decreasing in the U.S. labor market. Their data indicate that the disparity in jobless rates of young Black and White men, with and without a high school diploma, were not nearly as stark in the 1960s as in the 1980s (Bluestone, Stevenson, & Tilley, 1992). Rose et al. (1992) have compiled similar findings for the Milwaukee labor market. Thus, given these economic realities, it appears that the theories that purport to explain the deteriorating quality of life in inner-city communities need to be reexamined.

However, based on the view of underlying causes of current social problems noted above, policymakers, with widespread public support, have instituted a set of what some consider paternalistic and punitive public policies to "change welfare as we know it" and to foster normative behavior among the inner-city poor. In response to the high rates of lethal violence, for example, policymakers instituted a series of "get tough, lock them up and throw away the key" crime policies during the 1980s. To reduce welfare dependency and to foster responsibility and strengthen family values and morals, policies designed to teach the inner-city disadvantaged the importance of staying in school (*Learnfare*), of not having children until marriage (*Wedfare* and *Bridefare*), and of getting and maintaining a job (*Workfare*) have been implemented in many states and currently are being contemplated at the federal level.

There is a growing body of evidence which suggests that punitive and paternalistic policies may not yield the desired results. It has been documented that the "get tough" on crime policies of the 1980s have not significantly reduced the incidence of illegal and violent criminal activities in inner-city communities (Thomas, 1994), and it is doubtful that the U.S. economy can create enough good jobs to "change welfare as we know it."

An emerging school of thought posits that access to *social resources* is the key to the resolution of the pressing problems of the inner-city. According to Johnson, Oliver, and Bobo (1994), "social resources can be broadly defined as contacts through which the individual maintains his/her social identity and receives emotional support, material aid and services, information, and new social contacts" (p. 86). They note further that "such support can be obtained from individuals (e.g., immediate and extended family members, friends, co-ethnics, etc.) and/or institutions (e.g., churches, community based organizations, etc.)" (p. 86).

Historically, such community-based social resources as the Boys' and Girls' Clubs, the YMCA, and the YWCA played a "mediating" role in inner-city communities. They encouraged the inner-city disadvantaged, especially poor youth, to pursue mainstream avenues of social and economic mobility and discouraged them from engaging in antisocial or dysfunctional behavior. But during the 1980s, those mediating institutions lost much of their financial support and became less effective precisely at the time that the problems confronting the urban disadvantaged were worsening as a consequence of massive inner-city disinvestment on the part of major employers, financial institutions, and the federal government.

Milwaukee's Midnight Basketball League is one example of a new generation of social resource programs, *initiated and funded by the private sector,* which are designed to mend the social fabric of inner-city communities. The results of our program evaluation suggest that the "returns" on the money invested in *In the Paint at One Two* are far greater than the returns on the enormously popular punitive and paternalistic policies and programs advocated at all levels of government.

In the Paint at One Two, a $70,000 investment, reduced crime by 30% during the first year in the target area, according to Milwaukee Police Department statistics, and our survey indicates that the program (1) created a safe haven in which the participants (and the fans) could engage in positive social activities, (2) channeled the energy of gang members in a positive direction, and (3) significantly improved the educational and career aspirations of program participants.

How do the relative returns compare? The amount of money invested in Milwaukee's Midnight Basketball League would maintain two Black males in prison for roughly one year. One does not have to be an investment banker to realize that programs like the Midnight Basketball League will generate a much higher return in terms of human capital development than any or all of the punitive and paternalistic policies that currently garner so much political and media attention.

ACKNOWLEDGMENTS

The authors gratefully acknowledge the expert technical assistance of Ms. Cathy Mae Nelson of the University of Wisconsin-Milwaukee's School of Education word processing pool.

This research was supported by the Department of Educational Policy and Community Studies and the Office of Research, School of Education, University of Wisconsin-Milwaukee; the Piney Woods Country Life School, Piney Woods, Mississippi; Todd Robert Murphy Marketing Communications, Inc. and the Corporate Offices of Roundy's Foods, Milwaukee, WI; the Milwaukee Boys' and Girls' Club, Hillside Unit; the Milwaukee Police Department; and the Kenan Institute of Private Enterprise, University of North Carolina at Chapel Hill. The results and opinions do not necessarily reflect the position or policies of these institutions, and no official endorsement should be inferred.

REFERENCES

Bessone, L. T. (1992, November 15). Welcome to night court. *Sports Illustrated,* pp. 3-4.

Blueston, B., Stevenson, M. H., & Tilly, C. (1992). *An assessment of the impact of deindustrialization and spatial mismatch on the market outcomes of young White, Black, and Latino men and women who have limited schooling.* Boston: The John McCormick Institute of Public Affairs, University of Massachusetts at Boston.

Burkee, D. (1994, December 19). Memorandum on 1993 and 1994 scholarship awardees, In the Paint at One Two. Milwaukee, WI.

Children no more (Kids in crime, kids in gangs, kids in the system). (1992, August 24, 25, & 26). *Milwaukee Sentinel,* pp. 1A & 6A (daily).

Collins, C. M., & Cohen, D. (Eds.). (1993). *The African Americans.* New York: Viking Studio Books.

Cooper, K. J. (1994, November). Crime and punishment. *Emerge,* pp. 46-47.

Curry, J. (1990, February 6). Going to the hoop to redirect lives. *The New York Times,* p. 39.

Farrell, W. C., Jr., & Johnson, J. H., Jr. (1992, March 5). *Demographic overview of Milwaukee's core Black community within the context of three city areas.* Milwaukee, WI: Department of Educational Policy and Community Studies, University of Wisconsin-Milwaukee, Memorandum to Adorno & Zeder Law Firm.

Freking, K. (1992, May 2). Night basketball for LR teen-agers on board's agenda. *Arkansas Democrat Gazette,* p. 2B.

In a late night sport, the game is fighting crime. (1989, February 12). *The New York Times,* p. 51.

Johnson, J. H., Jr., Oliver, M. L., & Bobo, L. D. (1994). Understanding the contours of deepening inequality: Theoretical underpinnings and research design of a multi-city study. *Urban Geography, 15*(1), 77-89.

Laningham, S. (1991, July 31). Midnight basketball could begin in month. *Arkansas Democrat Gazette,* p. 9A.

Lott, T. (1992). Marooned in America: Black urban youth culture and social pathology. In B. E. Lawson (Ed.), *The Black underclass question* (pp. 71-89). Philadelphia: Temple University Press.

Midnight basketball credited in Phoenix crime reduction. (1994, August 19). *The Clarion-Ledger* (Jackson, MS), p. 7A.

New book, *The African Americans,* presents striking images of Black achievement. (1993, October). *Ebony,* pp. 122-123.

Rose, H. M., Edari, R. S., Quinn, L. M., & Pawasarat, J. (1992, November). *The labor market experience of young African American men from low-income families in Wisconsin.* Milwaukee, WI: Employment and Training Institute, Division of Outreach and Continuing Education Extension, University of Wisconsin-Milwaukee.

Schultze, S. (1993, July 22). City's Blacks fare worst in study. *Milwaukee Journal,* p. B4.

Tennille, G. (1994, July 10). Night court. *Arkansas Democrat Gazette,* pp. 8C & 10C.

Thomas, P. (1994, July 18-24). Getting to the bottom line on crime. *The Washington Post National Weekly Edition,* pp. 31-32.

Walker, K. (1991a, July 30). Inner-city midnight basketball discussed. *Arkansas Democrat Gazette,* p. 9A.

Walker, K. (1991b, July 31). Press is on for midnight basketball. *Arkansas Democrat Gazette,* p. 10A.

Will, G. F. (1990, October 18). City game. *Chicago Tribune,* p. 38.

Index

Page numbers followed by "f" indicate figures; page numbers followed by "t" indicate tables.

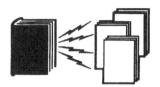

Haworth
DOCUMENT DELIVERY
SERVICE

This valuable service provides a single-article order form for any article from a Haworth journal.

- *Time Saving:* No running around from library to library to find a specific article.
- *Cost Effective:* All costs are kept down to a minimum.
- *Fast Delivery:* Choose from several options, including same-day FAX.
- *No Copyright Hassles:* You will be supplied by the original publisher.
- *Easy Payment:* Choose from several easy payment methods.

Open Accounts Welcome for . . .
- Library Interlibrary Loan Departments
- Library Network/Consortia Wishing to Provide Single-Article Services
- Indexing/Abstracting Services with Single Article Provision Services
- Document Provision Brokers and Freelance Information Service Providers

---

MAIL or *FAX* THIS ENTIRE ORDER FORM TO:

Haworth Document Delivery Service
The Haworth Press, Inc.
10 Alice Street
Binghamton, NY 13904-1580

or FAX: 1-800-895-0582
or CALL: 1-800-342-9678
9am-5pm EST

PLEASE SEND ME PHOTOCOPIES OF THE FOLLOWING SINGLE ARTICLES:

1) Journal Title: _____

    Vol/Issue/Year:_____Starting & Ending Pages:_____

Article Title:_____

_____

2) Journal Title: _____

    Vol/Issue/Year:_____Starting & Ending Pages:_____

Article Title:_____

_____

3) Journal Title: _____

    Vol/Issue/Year:_____Starting & Ending Pages:_____

Article Title:_____

_____

4) Journal Title: _____

    Vol/Issue/Year:_____Starting & Ending Pages:_____

Article Title:_____

(See other side for Costs and Payment Information)

COSTS: Please figure your cost to order quality copies of an article.

1. Set-up charge per article: $8.00
   ($8.00 × number of separate articles) _____

2. Photocopying charge for each article:

   1-10 pages: $1.00 _____

   11-19 pages: $3.00 _____

   20-29 pages: $5.00 _____

   30+ pages: $2.00/10 pages _____

3. Flexicover (optional): $2.00/article _____

4. Postage & Handling: US: $1.00 for the first article/
   $.50 each additional article _____

   Federal Express: $25.00 _____

   Outside US: $2.00 for first article/
   $.50 each additional article _____

5. Same-day FAX service: $.35 per page _____

GRAND TOTAL: _____

METHOD OF PAYMENT: (please check one)

❑ Check enclosed   ❑ Please ship and bill. PO # _____
(sorry we can ship and bill to bookstores only! All others must pre-pay)

❑ Charge to my credit card: ❑ Visa; ❑ MasterCard; ❑ Discover;
   ❑ American Express;

Account Number: _____ Expiration date: _____

Signature: *X* _____

Name: _____ Institution: _____

Address: _____

_____

City: _____ State: _____ Zip: _____

Phone Number: _____ FAX Number: _____

MAIL or *FAX* THIS ENTIRE ORDER FORM TO:

Haworth Document Delivery Service
The Haworth Press, Inc.
10 Alice Street
Binghamton, NY 13904-1580

or FAX: 1-800-895-0582
or CALL: 1-800-342-9678
        9am-5pm EST)

For Product Safety Concerns and Information please contact our
EU representative GPSR@taylorandfrancis.com Taylor & Francis
Verlag GmbH, Kaufingerstraße 24, 80331 München, Germany